The Great Alaska Nature Factbook

A Guide to the
State's Remarkable
Animals, Plants, and
Natural Features

Susan Ewing

ALASKA
NORTHWEST
BOOKS®

To Alaska dreamers, everywhere

Text copyright © 1996 by Susan Ewing
Illustrations copyright © 1996 by Robert Williamson

Revised Edition, 2011

Library of Congress Cataloging-in-Publication Data:

Ewing, Susan, 1954—
       The great Alaska nature factbook : a guide to the state's
   remarkable animals, plants, and natural features / by Susan Ewing.
           p. cm.
       Includes bibliographical references (p. 217) and index.
       ISBN 978-0-88240-838-5 (pbk.)
       ISBN 978-0-88240-988-7 (hardbound)
       ISBN 978-0-88240-868-2 (e-book)
1. Natural history—Alaska. I. Title.
   QH105.A4E95   1996
   508.798—dc20   95-47351
                                                        CIP

Formatter: Tracy Lamb
Illustrations: Robert Williamson
Map: Debbie Newell

Alaska Northwest Books®
An imprint of

GRAPHIC ARTS
BOOKS®
P.O. Box 56118
Portland, OR 97238-6118
(503) 254-5591
www.graphicartsbooks.com

CONTENTS

Acknowledgments

In many ways, a book such as this is more gathered than authored. Foraging for the facts contained here and preserving them in the spices of my own experience has been a real pleasure.

Responsibility for the end product, of course, rests with me, but I owe a great thanks to all those who helped me try to get it right. Special thanks to Jim Rearden for reviewing the entire manuscript, to Robert Armstrong for his review of birds and fishes, to Janice Schofield for her reading of the plant section, and to Carolyn Smith, tenacious and tireless editor.

For their comments and suggestions, corrections, and miscellaneous help, I would like to thank Misti Atkinson, Don Berry, Kathy Berry, Sue Ann Bowling, Alma Davis, Dr. Lawrence Duffy, Dr. Charles Geist, David Hopkins, Martin Jeffries, Charles E. Kline, Deborah Loop, Joy Martin, Michael McGowan, Jay McKendrick, Chris Nye, Charlotte Rowe, and Evon Zerbetz. Thanks also to the unnamed experts at the University of Alaska Fairbanks Geophysical Institute and elsewhere, who marked corrections in the margins of the passed-along pages crossing their desks.

Sincere thanks also to Ellen Wheat, former managing editor at Alaska Northwest Books®—developmental guiding hand for this writer as well as this book.

Alaska—

No Small Wonder

When I was still in high school, around 1970, I went with a friend for an afternoon drive in rural Kentucky. We stopped at a cafe for pie and began talking with the waitress, who had just come back from Alaska.

"It's soooooo big," she said softly. Her eyes kind of glazed over as she leaned on the lunch counter, staring out the plate glass window to the tameness of farm country. I never forgot the look on her face, and a few years later I went to find out for myself just how big. I spent a dozen years measuring: walking the frozen rivers of the Interior in winter and floating them in summer. Trolling for salmon and watching whales in Southeast. Making Christmas-night dump runs in Prudhoe Bay to see the ravens and arctic foxes gathered on garbage piles. Bathing in arctic hot springs while camped in the snow. Bumming plane rides and boat rides, figuring, figuring. Soooooo big.

How big? Big enough for grizzly bears and wolves. Big enough to welcome tens of millions of wild salmon back to their home streams every year, and big enough for those streams to still be flowing free and clean. Big enough to have hidden more than a thousand trumpeter swans while the Lower 48 population was plundered to sixty-nine. Big enough to encompass one-fifth the area of the contiguous United States, have six distinct geographical regions—each with differing climates, topography, plants, and animals—and accommodate over one hundred million acres of protected land. Big enough for a person to get lost in, in a good way.

Other states can guide you to their remaining wild areas, but Alaska doesn't *have* nature—Alaska *is* nature. You don't come here, or don't stay here, for the shopping. The mountains draw you and keep you, or the salt water; or the moose or salmon or bear. People are still guests upon the land here, each settlement separated from the faraway next one by vast distances filled with mountains, forests, rivers, lakes, and tundra.

Although people have dug, drilled, caught, and cut their ways in and out of "boom" times—furs, gold, fish, timber, and oil— Alaska's natural integrity has remained basically intact by force of its sheer size and inaccessibility. A mere fraction of the land has been directly altered by the human touch. With increasing demands for natural resources and the development of new technologies aimed at fulfilling those demands, along with a growing state population, the balance is poised to shift. But for now, rivers have the last say about their effect on the land, not dams, and— outside the cities—roadless is a way of life. Unlike the case in the vast majority of places in the Lower 48, Alaskan animals for the most part have not been squeezed out of their home territories; the ratio of pavement to raw land still favors ducks over developers. Oceanfront seabird nesting colonies far outnumber oceanfront resort condominiums along a coast that has more shoreline miles than the perimeter of the entire Lower 48. Small wonder Alaska is the last frontier for many species and habitat types that have disappeared or become rare in the Lower 48—from wolves to wetlands.

But contrary to the way it may appear, Alaska isn't all bigness and strength. While the Great Land is home to the largest mammals on earth—whales more than fifty feet long—it is also home to the smallest: pygmy shrews weighing less than a penny. In Southeast Alaska, thundering spruce trees reach heights of over two hundred feet while tiny orchids grow petitely at their bases.

More than being big and strong, Alaska's living things need to be adaptable. And being the rugged individualists they are, the state's natural citizens choose a variety of approaches for coping with the extremes of winter: ptarmigan turn camouflage white and stay active, while marmots and frogs hibernate and terns head south; tamarack trees lose their needles to keep from freeze-drying, and arctic plants grow in low, wind-resistant and heat-trapping mats close to the ground. The payoff for putting up with winter cold and dark is summer sunlight galore, abundant insect and berry food, water, and undisturbed expanses of land on which to have and raise offspring. Winter does have its virtues and even its pleasures, but it's hard to match—or measure—the complete perfection contained in one consummate summer day.

Whether you live in the Last Frontier or are just visiting, you'll find *The Great Alaska Nature Factbook* revealing reading about the animals, plants, and natural features that make Alaska such a remarkable, irreplaceable place. It's not meant to be a comprehensive field guide—think of it rather as an informal phrase book you can use to enhance your own conversations with the Great Land as you walk, float, fly, or motor through it, trying to see for yourself just how big it is.

Alaska's Geographic Regions

If we organized land according to features of geography or ecology, instead of politics or cartographic convenience, Alaska would be at least six states instead of one. To get an inkling of Alaska's environmental diversity and physical size, imagine California, Wisconsin, Missouri, Utah, Wyoming, Florida, and Louisana all lumped together under the same legislature.

On the same March day, it can be a damp 30°F in the old-growth forests of Southeast, a cold, dry –20°F on the Arctic tundra, and a sunny 11°F in the birch woodlands of the Interior. About 320 inches of snow fall each year on Valdez in Southcentral Alaska, while only 28 inches fall on Barrow in the Arctic. Fort Yukon in the Interior has seen 100°F summer days; a typical July day on the Alaska Peninsula in Southwestern Alaska may be 55°F.

Alaska's weather is greatly influenced by topography. Winds blowing from the ocean can supply coastal areas with warm air in the winter and cool air in the summer—moderating extremes of temperatures in those areas and creating a climate that is often cloudy, rainy, and windy. (Winter wind blowing off the Arctic Ocean and Chukchi Sea is cold, since those waters are frozen in the winter months.) Coastal mountains of Southcentral Alaska and the Alaska Range in the Interior act to hold rainy weather out

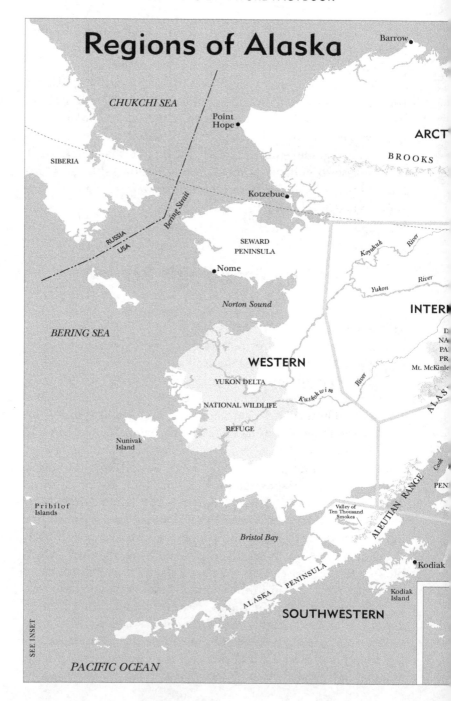

Regions of Alaska

Barrow

CHUKCHI SEA

Point
Hope

ARCT

SIBERIA

BROOKS

Kotzebue

Bering Strait

RUSSIA
USA

SEWARD
PENINSULA

Koyukuk   River

Nome

Yukon   River

Norton Sound

INTERI

BERING SEA

WESTERN

D
NA
PA
PR
Mt. McKinle

YUKON DELTA

NATIONAL WILDLIFE

Kuskokwim   River

REFUGE

ALASK

Nunivak
Island

Pribilof
Islands

Valley of
Ten Thousand
Smokes

Cook

PEN

ALEUTIAN RANGE

Bristol Bay

Kodiak

ALASKA PENINSULA

Kodiak
Island

SEE INSET

SOUTHWESTERN

PACIFIC OCEAN

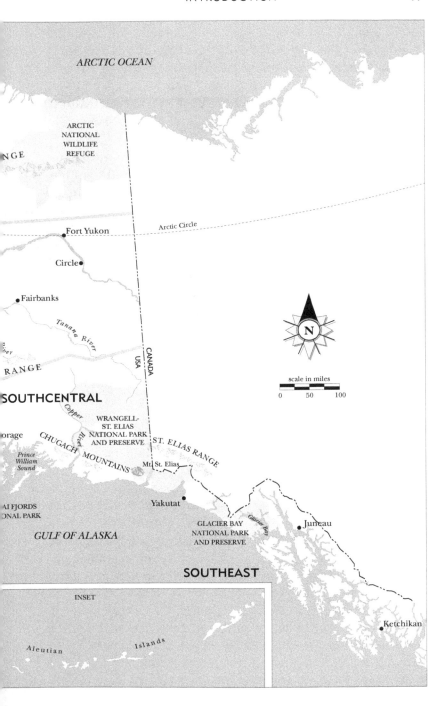

ARCTIC OCEAN

ARCTIC
NATIONAL
WILDLIFE
NGE REFUGE

Fort Yukon Arctic Circle

Circle

Fairbanks

Tanaga River

CANADA
USA

RANGE

SOUTHCENTRAL

Copper

WRANGELL-
ST. ELIAS
orage NATIONAL PARK ST. ELIAS RANGE
CHUGACH AND PRESERVE
Prince MOUNTAINS
William Mt. St. Elias
Sound

AI FJORDS Yakutat
NAL PARK
GLACIER BAY Juneau
GULF OF ALASKA NATIONAL PARK
AND PRESERVE

SOUTHEAST

N

scale in miles
0 50 100

INSET

Ketchikan

Aleutian Islands

of the Interior, at least when winds are from the south. West winds can bring wet weather in from the Bering Sea. In the north, the Brooks Range often protects the Interior from cold, arctic air masses.

Each of Alaska's regions—from the Arctic to Southeast—has its own distinct weather, wildlife, plant life, and personality.

Arctic Alaska The Arctic region is an immense, nearly road-less wilderness that stretches from the north slope of the Brooks Range to the coast of the Arctic Ocean. It is in the northern part of this region that taiga forests finally give way to flat or rolling tundra cut with countless rivers and small lakes. In the spring, insects and flowers rush to complete some portion of their life cycles in the short, intense growing season. Birds flock here by the millions to eat the insects and nest on the spongy ground. Precipitation in the Arctic is very low, but permanently frozen ground called permafrost keeps soils from draining, thus creating vast areas of wetlands. Moose browse the willows and other tundra vegetation, and large herds of caribou take advantage of the long daylight hours to feed and travel. Bowhead whales and bearded seals ply the summer waters of the Arctic Ocean, which is covered with ice the other nine months of the year.

In winter Arctic life is subdued, but it does go on, overseen by ravens, foxes, lemmings, snowy owls, and polar bears. Inupiaq and Yupik peoples were the original human settlers here; the Arctic town of Barrow is the largest Inupiaq community in the world. Thanks to a road built to supply the North Slope oil fields and trans-Alaska oil pipeline, it is possible to drive to the Arctic Coast.

Interior Alaska South of the Arctic region (but including land above the Arctic Circle), the huge Interior region extends southward from the Brooks Range to the Alaska Range, and from the Canadian border west about two-thirds of the way across the state. From its dais in the Alaska Range, Denali rules over the Interior landscape of rivers, hills, wet and dry tundra, muskeg, birch and spruce woodlands, aspen, alder, and tamarack trees. Bears hide in the ubiquitous willow; moose munch pond lilies; wolves lope the open country. The brawny Yukon River muscles through the region on its own schedule. Before gold miners and homesteaders arrived, the Interior belonged to the Athabascan Indians. Fairbanks, which today is Alaska's second-largest city, was incorporated in 1903.

Western Alaska
Alaska's Western region is flanked by the Interior on the east and the Chukchi and Bering Seas on the west. Extending from the Arctic Circle south to (but not including) the Alaska Peninsula, this land is covered mostly by treeless tundra, although parts of the Seward Peninsula and Bristol Bay areas are forested. Summer temperatures vary from the 30s to low 60s. Although windchill can lower temperatures significantly, winter days are usually in the 0°F to 30°F range. Yupik people were indigenous here and many still maintain their traditional subsistence hunting and fishing way of life. Millions of sockeye salmon—the largest sockeye run in the world—return to Western Alaska waters every year. And well over 102 million birds come to nest in the 19.6-million-acre Yukon Delta National Wildlife Refuge—the second-largest wildlife refuge in the United States, after the Arctic National Wildlife Refuge.

No roads lead to Western Alaska. A few roads do lead from place to place within the region, however—the seventy-two-mile gravel Nome to Teller road, for instance, is open from May through October. But if your destination lies within Western Alaska, you'll probably be getting there by plane or boat. Bethel, population 4,818, is the region's largest community.

Southwestern Alaska
Alaska's Southwestern region includes the Alaska Peninsula and the Aleutian Islands, which separate the Bering Sea to the north and the North Pacific Ocean to the south. The Peninsula's mountainous spine and the thousand-mile-long chain of more than two hundred islands are slowly being formed as the Pacific tectonic plate dives below Alaska at this famous section of the actively volcanic Pacific Rim of Fire. Sitka alder is abundant on the Peninsula, but the Aleutians are treeless, grown over in luxuriant grass instead. Known as the "birthplace of the winds," the Aleutian Islands harbor weather that has been called the worst in the world. Temperatures are moderate

enough—20s in the winter, 50s in the summer—but wind and rain-storms can be ferocious. Attu, farthest island at the end of the Aleutian Chain, is a thousand miles distant from Unimak Island, situated at the end of the Alaska Peninsula.

Brown bears are abundant on the Peninsula, and seabirds come by the millions to nest throughout the region, which includes the Pribilof Islands. Sea otters once again flourish on the south side of the Alaska Peninsula, as they did in times past, when they drew the attention of the first foreign fur traders. Aleut people were standing on the shore when the Russians landed in the eighteenth century.

Southcentral Alaska
Anchorage is the social hub of Southcentral Alaska, a region that is home to two-thirds of the state's population. From the Gulf of Alaska in the south to the Alaska Range in the north, and from the Chugach Mountains in the east to the Aleutian Range to the west, Southcentral Alaska holds a varied mix of habitat, terrain, and animal types. The maritime climate is moderate, but with tastes of dryer, colder Interior influences in the region's northern reaches.

Southcentral features high mountains, broad valleys, climax forests, world-renowned wetlands, and inland woodlands of aspen and birch—and brown bears, mountain goats, Dall sheep, moose, lynx, beavers, birds, and their myriad kith and kin all find a niche here somewhere. The first human niche in this region was filled by Athabascan and Sugpiaq peoples.

Southeast Alaska
Southeast Alaska—the Panhandle—lies docked up against British Columbia like a flotilla of forested icebergs. Steep, wet, green, dense, and lush, about three quarters of Southeast lies within the Tongass National Forest, the largest in the United States. Thick old-growth stands of Sitka spruce and western hemlock grow right down to the waterline. The Inside Passage, a corridor of sheltered salt water, provides a marine highway through Southeast—a good thing, since only three Alaskan communities (Haines, Hyder, and Skagway) in this five-hundred-mile-long strip are connected to anywhere by road. Every other place, including Ketchikan and Juneau (the state capital), can be

reached only by boat or airplane. Native peoples of Southeast—Eyak, Tlingit, Haida and Tsimshian—traveled in dugout canoes built of huge cedar logs.

Annual precipitation in some areas of Southeast can reach two hundred inches. Winter temperatures are moderate, hovering around freezing in the snowy, rainy cold season. Summers are generally cool. Devil's club grows thick in Southeast, as do berry bushes, ferns, and moss. Southeast is prime territory for Sitka black-tailed deer, whales, porpoises, and mountain goats. The largest and most famous gathering of bald eagles in the world happens in this region near the town of Haines, timed around a fall run of salmon.

ONE

Animals

MORE CARIBOU live in Alaska than people—and more salmon and more seabirds, and certainly more mosquitoes. The Great Land is home to 105 species of mammals, more than 430 kinds of fish, nearly 300 birds, insects by the net load, seven amphibians, and a couple of transient reptiles in the form of sea turtles. And thanks to a wide variety of habitats, Alaska's animals are a surprisingly diverse lot: areas from old-growth forest to arctic tundra provide niche accommodations for everything from banana slugs to polar bears.

While wildlife in the Forty-ninth State is abundant, don't expect animals to be covering every foot. It takes a lot of territory to support a herd of caribou, a pack of wolves, or an Interior grizzly bear. The forage available for the grazing animals—which in turn become meals for the predators—is far less sustaining and sustainable than were the grasslands and oak woodlands that once supported huge bison herds and flocks of passenger pigeons in the Lower 48. But what Alaska land lacks in square meals, it more than makes up for in square miles. And more than one hundred million acres—fifty-six million of which are designated wilderness—are protected and managed with the needs of wildlife and habitat in mind.

While Alaska has much to offer wildlife in the way of undisturbed space, the deal does come with a price: winter. Strategies for survival are as varied as the species and habitats themselves. All of Alaska's terrestrial mammals stay in the state year-round (with the exception of bats, which are relatively uncommon in the state, generally limited to Southeast, and thought mostly to migrate south in the winter). Some of Alaska's mammals, most notably caribou, do migrate, but their migration is from location to location within state borders.

Mammals—warm-blooded animals whose metabolisms perpetuate a relatively constant body temperature—must eat more as weather cools to fuel their metabolism furnaces. So the warm-blooded creatures who remain active in the cold season—including foxes, moose, mice, polar bears, ravens, and snowy owls—must have an adequate food supply. Voles and mice, who may spend nearly the entire winter under the insulating cover of snow, huddled together in family groups for warmth, tunnel runways to uncover grasses to eat. The pika plans ahead, spending the summer collecting grass and other plants to dry for use as winter food. Small furbearers such as these provide a good prey base for foxes, owls, and weasels.

Most warm-blooded mammals put on weight and grow heavier coats in preparation for winter, but there are also other, more customized adaptations. In some large herbivores such as caribou and musk oxen, special nasal passages are designed to capture heat that would otherwise escape as steamy breath, and to transfer the warmth to the animal's blood. Arctic wolves have specialized blood vessels in their paws that keep pad temperatures about 1°F above freezing to prevent snow from melting and then refreezing into toe-jamming ice balls.

Some winter residents avoid the whole climate challenge by hibernating. Marmots, ground squirrels, and those brown and black bears who hibernate dramatically reduce their internal temperatures and body functions and snooze in underground burrows or dens where temperatures won't drop below freezing.

Why do warm-blooded animals put up with the cold? Because even in winter, there is still enough food and burrow room to support a few extra members of the species. After all, an appropriate number of permanent residents keeps an ecosystem in equilibrium—like a skeleton crew on the job to keep things functioning during the slack season.

Birds, which are also warm-blooded, don't hibernate. Unlike the stay-at-home mammals, more than two-thirds of Alaska's birds migrate out of state for the winter, returning in the spring from as far away as Africa, Antarctica, Asia, Hawaii, South America, and Australia.

Although some small birds, such as chickadees, do stay in Alaska for the winter, they're the exceptions. It has been found that birds living in the north have higher standard metabolic rates than do other members of the same species living in more moderate climates. Lack of a reliable food supply drives most birds south in the winter, but summer brings them back for the bounty of insects, seeds, berries, fish, aquatic plants, and mudflat organisms. Upon their return, birds find not only food, but also plenty of undisturbed nesting space.

Summertime Alaska is a bird banquet. Arctic nesters feed on thick swarms of insects, and migrating seabirds stop off to fatten up in the food-rich waters of the Bering Sea and North Pacific before moving on to nest elsewhere. Increased daylight hours allow plenty of time for eating, breeding, and finding a nest site.

Alaska also has cold-blooded animals, which don't generate their own internal heat. Interestingly, cold-blooded (poikilothermic) animals—including fish, amphibians, and invertebrates—can generally survive sustained colder temperatures than can warm-blooded (homoiothermic) animals. Cold-blooded animals that have adapted to cold climates move toward a sort of suspended animation as temperatures drop. Requiring little food, they bide their time until conditions are more favorable before becoming active again. There are northern insects that can actually freeze and come back to life, and some arctic fish have an antifreeze-like substance in their body tissues.

But not all cold-blooded animals are cut out for life in the Northland. Snakes and lizards can't survive in Alaska because they rely on the warmth of direct sunshine to keep themselves going and hatch their eggs.

Habitat is the key to finding and knowing wildlife. The more you know about an animal's habitat requirements—what it needs in terms of food, space, water, and cover—the better your chances of observing creatures in their natural surroundings. You wouldn't expect to find chickadees, which nest in holes in dead trees, on the treeless tundra. But you could anticipate finding sandhill cranes or snowy owls, both of which nest on the ground.

Biologists have identified fourteen distinct wildlife habitats in Alaska:

- the hemlock–spruce forests, which cover most of Southeast and include old-growth temperate rain forest
- the spruce–hardwood forests in the Interior
- scattered tall-shrub thickets of alder, willow, and birch
- muskeg

- the alpine tundra above tree line and on lower, exposed ridges
- the moist tundra of lowlands and river basins
- water-soaked wet tundra with patches of permanent standing water
- freshwater rivers and lakes and their shorelines
- coastal wetlands, including river deltas, mudflats, salt marshes, and sandy beaches
- the barrier islands and lagoons of Alaska's northern and western coasts
- the rocky shores and cliffs of coastal islands
- marine waters, including the unique ecological zone created by pack ice
- glaciers and ice fields
- human-altered habitats

As long as its ecosystems remain intact, the Great Land will continue to support a rich repository of wildlife. Alaska is the last frontier for many species that are now rare in, or completely gone from, historical ranges in the Lower 48—wolves, grizzly bears, grayling, lynx, peregrine falcons, wolverines, and others. With patience, planning, and a little luck, you may see some of these special animals. But even if you don't see a wolf or a bear or a falcon, look for its shadow on the land; imagine it there. It might be looking at you.

ARCTIC CHAR If the Salmonidae family threw a reunion, arctic char's invitation would need the most postage. The troutlike fish *(Salvelinus alpinus)* ranges even beyond Alaska, to Ellesmere Island, Northwest Territories—a place nearly at the top of the world. Although arctic char in other parts of North America sometimes take to the sea, Alaska's char are strictly lake residents, living in lakes of the Brooks Range, Kodiak Island, Kenai Peninsula, the Alaska Peninsula, Bristol Bay region, and in a small area near Denali National Park and Preserve.

Char are a subgroup within the extended salmon family, which includes Dolly Varden, the arctic char's closest relation. Arctic char were critical to Northern people, including the Inuit of Canada, who harvested the fish using stone weirs and spears made from musk ox horns and polar bear bones.

Arctic char have the standard salmon/trout streamlined body shape, but their coloring and size vary widely, depending on the time of year, age of the fish, and in what lake the fish is living. In general, char are brownish olive with light-colored spots on their sides, and can weigh anywhere from one or two pounds to over ten. Some of the biggest char in the state live in large lakes around the Bristol Bay area—a favorite destination of many resident and nonresident sport anglers. Fishing for this piscine prize is best from May through early July when arctic char gather to feed on juvenile salmon moving out to sea.

See also DOLLY VARDEN

ARCTIC FOX Depending on what the situation calls for, this smallest of the Northland canines can be a hunter, scavenger, berry eater, or hoarder. In spring and summer when prey animals are plentiful, arctic foxes are known to cache surplus catches of seabirds and rodents to eat when the lean season comes.

Alaska's arctic foxes live in treeless coastal areas from the Aleutian Islands north to the Arctic coast. These plucky foxes aren't very territorial and will simply move on in search of better pickings when food becomes scarce. They may even follow polar bears out onto the ice pack in hopes of feasting on a bear's leftover seal. Arctic foxes can travel great distances over sea ice; one fox radio-tagged on the Russian coast was located a year later on the north coast of Alaska near Wainwright.

For their size (six to ten pounds), arctic foxes have the thickest fur of any polar animal. *Alopex lagopus* comes in two color forms, white and "blue." The white form is common in the Far North, while blue arctic foxes are more common on the Aleutian and Pribilof Islands. Even though the two forms can be born into the same litter, blue arctic foxes remain charcoal-colored all their lives, while white foxes molt with the seasons, turning brownish in the summer and white again each winter. Both white and blue forms are born with dark, velvety fur, and both have the arctic fox's trademark long bushy tail and short legs and ears.

Arctic foxes can kill significant numbers of seabird adults and eat many eggs. Wolves help keep fox populations in check, as do human trappers. Although the fur trade has diminished, the sale of fox pelts still provides important income to many Alaska Natives and nonnative trappers.

BEARS Bear—a small word for such a large presence, not only in the physical sense (brown bears can weigh over a thousand pounds) but also in the abstract sense: knowing you're in bear country makes for prickly sensations of anticipation, excitement, and heightened awareness.

Bears are as much a part of the Alaska landscape as trappers' cabins and blueberries, which is not to say they should be taken for granted. If you'll be in the backcountry, learn how to avoid bear encounters and how to protect yourself. Both black bears and brown bears can be dangerous, although far more people die of hypothermia than from a bear attack. And fortunately, chances of an unpleasant encounter are slim. But chances of seeing a bear from the safety of a car, boat, or small airplane are pretty decent, and pretty exciting.

Black Bear Black bears (*Ursus americanus*) are widespread in most forested areas of Alaska south of the Brooks Range. Black bears are at least 50 percent smaller than browns; males average about two hundred pounds, females are about 20 percent smaller.

Color isn't a good clue in distinguishing black bears from browns since black bears can range from black through cinnamon brown to blond. The rare "glacier bears" occasionally seen near Yakutat are bluish gray. Size isn't that good a clue either, since a black bear can look pretty darn big in certain situations. To tell black bears from brown, look at the face and shoulders: a black bear has a sort of Roman profile, whereas the face of a grizzly appears wide and slightly dished; black bears also lack the distinctive shoulder hump noticeable on brown bears.

> Black bears have a Roman profile and lack the distinctive shoulder hump of the grizzly.

The claws of black bears are another clue. You shouldn't be close enough to see that kind of detail in person, but you can read the tracks. The claws of black bears are short and curved, so claw prints are close to the pad print. Claw prints in a grizzly track reach farther forward.

Black bear claws aren't much good for digging, but they're just right for climbing trees, which the bears commonly do to escape danger. Because black bears evolved in the forest and grizzlies originally adapted to open country, black bears tend to defend themselves by climbing or hiding, whereas grizzlies developed aggressive, stand-and-fight attitudes. Alaskans say that one way to tell whether you're being chased by a grizzly bear or a black bear is that a black bear will climb the tree after you and a grizzly bear will stay at the bottom and shake you out.

Like brown bears, black bears hibernate during the winter, and cubs are born in the den. Black bears also eat fish and will occasionally prey on newborn moose and deer, but their diet is at least 80 percent vegetarian, consisting mostly of berries, grasses, and clovers, supplemented by insects, carrion, and garbage. Wolves, humans, grizzly bears, and other black bears may sometimes prey on *U. americanus*.

Brown, or Grizzly, Bear

Brown bears and grizzly bears are the same species, *Ursus arctos*. Whether *Ursus arctos* is called "grizzly" or

"brownie" is often a matter of where the bear lives and what the locals prefer to call it. Generally speaking, "brown" bears live near the coast and supplement their diet with lots of fish and other protein-rich food, on which they grow quite large. The huge brown bears of Kodiak Island are considered a geographically isolated subspecies of brown bear, *U. arctos middensorffi.*

Coastal brown bears, which can weigh well over one thousand pounds and stand nine feet tall on their hind legs, are the largest omnivorous land mammals in the world. (Although similar in size to the brown bear, polar bears are considered marine mammals.)

"Grizzlies" are typically considered to be brown bears that live one hundred miles or more inland and eat a larger percentage of nonmeat foods such as berries, roots, and grasses—although many Alaskans simply call all *Ursus arctos* "brown" regardless of where they live.

Brown bears, which can actually be pale blond to almost black, are found in every region of Alaska. They are creatures of open country, preferring meadows and tundra to forests. When available, fish is the preferred food, but on average, bears eat far more vegetation than meat; plant foods make up about 70 percent of the diet of an average Interior grizzly. The claws of *Ursus arctos* are long and nearly straight—perfect for digging roots, bulbs, insects, and ground squirrels out of the ground. The pronounced shoulder hump is actually a powerful muscle the bear uses in digging.

Ursus arctos preys on newborn moose, caribou, and deer, but after the young ones are up and running, most bears go back to fishing, foraging, scavenging, and opportunistic preying on the occasional weakling. Some individual bears do become predatory, but they are the exception. Both brown bears and black bears are essentially herbivores with leftover canine teeth and latent carnivorous tendencies.

Most grizzly bears hibernate during the winter, but in coastal areas such as Kodiak Island or parts of Southeast, where the weather is relatively mild and food may be available all winter, bears might stay active all year.

Females give birth to cubs during hibernation. For so large an animal, gestation is short—about six months—and the one or two cubs are born hairless and with their eyes closed, weighing less than a pound. Drowsily, the sow bites through the umbilical cords, licks the babies, and goes back to sleep. The cubs spend the next few months huddled against their sleeping mother, suckling and growing. When it's time to leave the den in the spring, the cubs are fully developed. Cubs stay with the sow for at least a year and a half, sometimes longer. They never have contact with the boar, their male parent, who would just as soon eat them as look at them. Predation isn't much of a problem to *Ursus arctos*, but humans and other bears do kill bears, and wolves have been known to prey on cubs.

POLAR BEAR Polar bears are so closely associated with the sea—especially sea ice—that they are classified as marine mammals. The sleek white bears (*U. maritimus*, or "sea bear") are solitary wanderers, drifting with the ice pack in search of prey. With their narrow heads, long necks, and partially webbed feet, polar bears are tireless swimmers, and a generous fat layer keeps them warm in frigid waters.

Where black and brown bears have developed omnivorous appetites, the polar bear is the ultimate carnivore, stalking ringed seals at their breathing holes in the ice and occasionally nabbing beluga whales or other marine mammals. The bear's sharp claws, strength, stealth, speed, and size—up to 10 feet long and over a thousand pounds—make it one of the animal kingdom's most imposing predators.

While brown and black bears are hibernating, male and non-pregnant female polar bears go open-eyed into the winter: wandering, watching, hunting. Pregnant females den up in late October or November and emerge with cubs in late March or early April.

Listed as a threatened species under the US Endangered Species Act, Alaska's polar bears are divided into two geographic groups. The Beaufort Sea population, which is shared with Canada, is estimated at about 1,500 bears, and the Chukchi/ Bering Sea population numbers around 2,000. Both populations are declining, largely because of dwindling sea ice; arctic ice was at a record low in January 2011. Not only does a shrinking ice pack rob the bear of its hunting platform and access to sea-going prey, but studies show that reduced sea ice also affects polar bear reproductive rates. Worst-case scenarios project that polar bears could be extinct by 2050.

See also SEA ICE

BEAVER Beavers are the Clark Kents of the animal world. Shy and unassuming, the beaver is in truth a formidable force, influencing the landscape more than any other nonhuman animal. With self-sharpening, perpetually renewing incisors and unstoppable stick-to-it-iveness, beavers create ponds and wetlands for themselves and, consequently, for other animals; the sound of flowing water throws them into tizzy of purpose: dam it, dam it, dam it.

> The beaver influences the landscape more than any other animal besides humans.

The three- to four-foot-long, forty- to seventy-pound animals need two to three feet of water to feel secure from such predators as wolves and bears. And if they can't find a pond deep enough, these largest of North American rodents will make one, calling upon their impressive construction and engineering skills. Dams are typically ten to fifty feet long and three to five feet high. Sometimes working in teams, beavers begin a dam by securing downed trees into the mud of the stream bottom, parallel to the current, with the butt end facing upstream. The interlacing upper branches provide an infrastructure into which sticks and other material can be integrated. Tires, fishing rods, rags, antlers, and moose skeletons have all been found woven into beaver dams. Holes are plastered with mud, rock, grass, and roots that beavers carry to the dam in armloads held between their chin and front paws.

The clever problem solvers also build canals—which can be hundreds of feet long, several feet deep, and several feet wide—to reach trees not adjacent to their pond. The canals provide safe travel for the beaver and easy transport for the felled trees. A beaver can chew down a five-inch-diameter tree in under thirty minutes—slower than a speeding bullet, but nevertheless impressive. The herbivorous beaver will eat only the bark, using the stripped log for dam or lodge building. (Beavers also eat aquatic plants, roots, and grasses.) With its abundance of delectable construction materials such as willow, alder, aspen, and birch, Alaska is beaver heaven: *Castor canadensis* can be found near streams and rivers in all but the treeless Far North and some extreme western areas of the state.

Unlike most of its rodent relatives, the beaver is not very prolific and has stable, long-term family relationships. Pairs may stay together for their ten-year life span, having one litter of four or fewer kits a year. Two generations of young may live in the family lodge at any one time. Older kits help care for young and work with the parents to keep the lodge and dam in good repair. Beaver homes may be freestanding stick lodges or dens dug into the bank of faster-flowing rivers. In both types, there is a "family room" chamber where the animals sleep and an underwater entrance that also serves as a sort of mud room where a returning beaver can pause and allow water to drain from its thick fur.

In the fall, beavers cache fresh branches underwater in the pond to serve as a winter food supply. When the surface freezes, the beavers—who do not hibernate—can slip into the water through a submerged entrance and retrieve a meal; their body heat keeps the underwater access from freezing.

BELTED KINGFISHER Perhaps the belted kingfisher should be called the belted queenfisher—it is one of the few bird species in North America in which the female has more color than the male. Bigger than a robin but smaller than a crow, both male and female are easy to recognize by the oversized blue-gray head; sharp, heron-like beak; blue-gray back, wings, and breast band; white throat collar; and white belly. Females accessorize with a cummerbund of rusty orange.

King or queen, these birds rule the rivers—or at least so it seems; they announce their presence with a loud, rattling call, and can be very territorial when defending feeding territories. Kingfishers catch fish by diving in the water headfirst. After snatching a live one, the birds are known to return to a favorite perch, beat the fish against a limb, then toss the stunned fish into the air and swallow it headfirst.

Also found around lakes and protected bays, belted kingfishers *(Ceryle alcyon)*, the only kingfisher species found in Alaska, winter along the state's southern coast. In the spring and summer they range throughout all but the northernmost parts of Alaska. Nests are three- to seven-foot-long tunnels, three to four inches in diameter, excavated together by both male and female in sandy, clayey, or gravelly banks; sites are often chosen for their proximity to good fishing spots.

Belted Kingfisher

The species name *alcyon* derives from Halcyone, daughter of the Greek wind god. After her husband drowned, Halcyone threw herself into the sea to be near him. Taking pity on the lovers, the gods turned them into kingfishers, and declared that the winds cease blowing for a week before and after the winter solstice—a time that, in the Mediterranean, coincides with kingfisher nesting. The phrase "halcyon days" to describe times of peace and calm comes from this legend.

BISON Oh, give me a home, in the ice under Nome. . . . Until they were reintroduced to the state in 1928, the only bison in Alaska were packed in permafrost under the soil. Thousands of years ago, however, bison were the most common large land mammals around. Bison remains are among the most abundant large-animal relics found in the Interior, followed by woolly mammoth and prehistoric horse remains.

Alaska wasn't always a land of snow and ice; during periodic ice ages tens of thousands of years ago, parts of what are now Alaska and Canada remained ice-free, providing a rich grassland habitat for ancient grazing animals. But cold spells brought on by a changing global climate, combined perhaps with increasingly effective hunting techniques of early peoples, led to the bison's disappearance from the Northland more than ten thousand years ago.

Because Alaska is now more tundra than grassland, large populations of bison can no longer be supported, but bison on a smaller scale appear to be doing fine. At last count, about nine hundred roamed the state—all descendants of the original twenty animals transplanted from Montana to the Delta Junction area of the Interior. Alaska's modern bison, *Bison bison*, is a different species than the ancient steppe bison, *Bison priscus*.

Great Land bison aren't found in one giant herd, but have spread out naturally and through relocation programs. In addition to the Delta Junction herd, wild bison can be found singly or in groups along the Chitina and Copper Rivers and near Farewell. Domestic herds have been established near Healy and Kodiak.

Bison may seem docile and slow, but a Delta Junction bull was seen leaping a seven-foot log fence from a standing start.

See also BERINGIA; HORNS AND ANTLERS; WOOLLY MAMMOTH AND BLUE BABE

BITING FLIES If Alaskans could redesign themselves, they might start with steel skin. Along with mosquitoes, humans in the North Country must contend with a voracious array of biting insects, including black flies (*Simulium* spp.), no-see-ums (*Culicoides* spp.), and deer flies (*Chrysops* spp.). From spring breakup to fall freeze—all across Alaska—something is biting somewhere.

Like little Countesses Dracula, black fly females slice away a plug of skin from their victim and lap up the blood; males prefer flower nectar. Whitesox, as they're also called, are determined to get off a good bite, and may crawl under clothing or into a person's hair or ears to do so; bites often induce swelling and itching that may last for a week. These ¹⁄₁₆- to ¼-inch-long flies have a distinctive humpbacked shape and are found near running water in forests, mountains, and tundra.

> **Black fly females slice away a plug of skin from their victim and lap up the blood.**

No-see-ums look like miniature mosquitoes. In a swarm, the silver-winged gnats can drive you crazy with their unrelenting, unlady-like nips (like the black fly, only the female bites). The ¹⁄₁₆- to ⅛-inch-long "punkies" are most noticeable around ponds and streams.

If you're ever bitten by a deer fly you may wonder if this broad-headed, bug-eyed bloodsucker isn't actually a carnivore. Active all summer, the bee-sized deer fly also has other common names, most of which are unprintable. It should by now come as no surprise that only the females bite.

To avoid Alaska's biting bugs you can stay in downtown Anchorage, or on a boat far from shore, or on a glacier, or in the wind—or you can go outside only when temperatures are below freezing. But if you venture into the bush or anywhere off the beaten path near freshwater lakes, ponds, or streams during spring, summer, or fall, be prepared. Insect repellent isn't very effective with biting flies, so cover up with elastic-cuffed clothing.

Although any bite can become infected if not kept clean, Alaska's biting flies aren't considered a health threat (unless perhaps you include mental health).

What good are biting flies? Each one of these species spends the larval stage of its life in the water—providing an important link in the freshwater food chain. Fish and other vertebrates eat the insect larvae; birds and mammals eat the fish. So the next time you eat fish from an Alaskan river or lake, you can thank a biting fly.

BLACKFISH On the outside the blackfish—found only in Alaska and eastern Siberia—is unremarkable: a flat-headed, round-tailed bottom fish with dark blotchy skin. But beneath the blackfish's uninspired veneer lies an extraordinary esophagus. Only one other fish in the world, a tropical swamp eel, comes with such equipment, specialized to allow the fish to breath air.

Because they are able to absorb oxygen from the air, blackfish can survive in near-stagnant ponds, lakes, and rivers. They can even live for periods of time in nothing more than moist moss while waiting for rains to refill tundra pools.

Blackfish *(Dallia pectoralis)* are found throughout Western Alaska from the Arctic to the Alaska Peninsula and in the Interior's Yukon–Tanana drainage. Usually abundant where they do occur, blackfish have been a valuable subsistence fish. Some Alaska Native peoples call it *oonyeeyh*, meaning "to sustain life." Blackfish can be kept alive in tubs of water or covered with snow until they are needed.

Stories abound about the fish's hardiness. According to an 1886 account, a sled dog that had swallowed a whole, frozen blackfish later regurgitated it alive. Contemporary research has shown that blackfish can survive for up to forty minutes at temperatures of -4°F, and they can live for a few days after being partially frozen. *Oonyeeyh* are also able to tolerate a total lack of oxygen for up to twenty-four hours if the temperature is precisely at freezing.

Blackfish, which are seldom longer than eight inches, feed on aquatic insects and other small invertebrates, and will also eat juvenile northern pike. In turn, blackfish are preyed upon by adult northern pike, burbot, river otters, mink, loons—and humans and sled dogs.

BURBOT They've been called mud shark, eel pout, lush, and lawyer—perhaps because of their looks and habits: *Lota lota* has a big, downturned mouth, a flat head, a single chin whisker, blotchy skin, and a long, almost eel-like body, and is a voracious predator that often eats its own young. A less colorful but still descriptive common name is freshwater ling, a reference to its physical similarity to the oceangoing lingcod. Whatever you call this fish, call it to dinner—it looks great on a plate. Eating burbot is one of the finer rewards of ice fishing.

Burbot, the only true freshwater cod, are found from polar regions to as far south as the Mississippi River drainage. In Alaska, the fish live in most of the state's larger rivers and many of its lakes, and are particularly widespread in the Interior; burbot prefer deep water and, even in rivers, will seek out the deepest pools.

The brownish green fish, which can reach weights over twenty pounds, are no-nonsense predators, feeding on all kinds of fish and other prey including mice and shrews unlucky enough to be swimming by. Burbot have even been caught with bank swallows in their stomachs; the birds may have been gobbled while skimming insects from the water's surface.

Unlike salmon, grayling, and many other fish, burbot do not spawn in pairs. Instead, large groups of males and females gather into a crowded, wiggling mass and release sperm and tiny eggs over sand or gravel. This isn't easy to witness since spawning takes place in the winter under the ice. Burbot have blood that is highly efficient at taking oxygen from water, so the fish can operate quite well in low-oxygen conditions, such as cold winter waters.

BUTTERFLIES Alaska's short, cool summers do more to limit the number of butterflies than do the harsh winters. For example, even though Southeast has milder winters than most other areas of Alaska, the summers aren't very sunny, so only about six of the state's eighty butterfly species live in Alaska's mild but cloudy panhandle.

Sun is the key ingredient in good butterfly habitat. Although Colorado has cold, snowy winters, it also has warm, sunny summers—and 250 butterfly species.

Because butterflies don't generate their own body heat, they rely on the sun to energize flight muscles and keep their bodies warm enough to incubate eggs. Northern species tend to be dark and small in order to most efficiently absorb and retain heat from the sun.

Butterflies go through four distinct stages of development: egg, caterpillar, pupa or chrysalis, and adult. In Alaska, the full life cycle of some butterfly species may take years to complete because the warm growing season is so short. In species that overwinter as adults, a natural antifreeze prevents body tissues from damage while the insects wait for spring in a sort of suspended animation.

One Alaskan butterfly shares its name with a famous northern fish: the arctic grayling *(Oeneis bore)*. This gray-brown, winged grayling is thought to have actually benefited from construction of the trans-Alaska oil pipeline, which increased the amount of bare, stony land on which this butterfly prefers to bask.

Like the arctic grayling, polixenes arctic *(Oeneis polixenes)* is strictly a northern species, living on wind-swept tundra above tree line. When polixenes alights, it often clasps its nearly translucent gray-brown wings together and bends them close to the ground, a posture that exposes more wing area to the warmth of the sun and helps the butterfly keep a low profile in the wind.

> In Alaska, the full life cycle of some butterfly species may take years to complete.

The dingy arctic fritillary *(Clossiana improba)* solves the high tundra wind and low solar energy problems by simply walking where it needs to go. This drab brown butterfly crawls more than it flies. Even as it crawls over tundra plants, this fritillary is still fulfilling its important butterfly role as plant pollinator.

CARIBOU In Alaska, caribou still outnumber people. About twenty-five more-or-less distinct herds are distributed across the state, including the 123,000-animal Porcupine herd that ranges in the Arctic National Wildlife Refuge. The Western arctic herd alone numbers 350,000 animals—73,000 more

Caribou

individuals than live in the municipality of Anchorage. Smaller herds exist throughout Northern Alaska and the Interior, bringing the caribou grand total to about 900,000.

Barren ground caribou *(Rangifer tarandus)* are well adapted for life on the open tundra. Their flat, broad two-toed hooves work like snowshoes in the winter and support the caribou over wet, spongy tundra in summer. The hooves also come in handy as paddles for swimming rivers and as shovels for pawing through the snow to find food. Northern peoples called caribou "the digging ones." Caribou graze on a wide variety of plants including willow leaves, seasonal grasses, and lichens.

A caribou's coarse coat can grow to be nearly two inches thick in the winter, each hair a hollow cylinder of insulating air. Hollow hair also provides added buoyancy for swimming. For its weight, the caribou's coat is said to be among the most well-insulated and windproof of fur—so efficient, in fact, that caribou are in danger of overheating on warm summer days. Oddly enough, antlers are important in summer heat regulation— perhaps this is one reason caribou are the only member of the deer family in which both male and female have antlers. Antlers are shed and regrown each year. In the early stages of growth, the new antlers are covered with a velvetlike skin. Blood flowing in veins through the velvet skin radiates away excess heat, helping cool the animal.

Smaller than moose and larger than Sitka black-tailed deer, caribou bulls weigh an average of 350 to 400 pounds; cows are generally about 30 percent smaller and generally have smaller antlers. With their rangy paddled-and-spiked antlers, white necks, and long regal faces, caribou are among the most stately looking of all ungulates (hoofed mammals).

Caribou migrations are one of North America's most awesome remaining natural spectacles. Sometimes traveling in the tens of thousands, they march from wintering areas to calving grounds, cows leading the way. After calving, they continue to drift, grazing an area for a while, then moving to fresh range. Herds can travel up to nine hundred miles from winter range to calving grounds to summer feeding areas.

See also HORNS AND ANTLERS; REINDEER

CHICKADEE *Chick-a-dee-dee-dee.* These small, busy birds are happy to introduce themselves when they come calling at a winter feeder—very happy indeed. At extremely low temperatures, chickadees must eat about twenty times more than usual to maintain their body heat and stay alive. Feeder treats such as sunflower seeds, suet, and fatty meat make life easier on these year-round Alaska residents, and the cheerful sight of chickadees in winter can make life easier on housebound human residents too, many of whom enjoy watching the avian troupers swoop from tree to feeder to tree.

After a day of eating, chickadees spend a cold night in a state of controlled hypothermia, maintaining lowered body temperatures with periodic fits of shivering. Flocks of six to a dozen birds—composed of one or two established pairs, some newly paired juveniles, and a few "floaters"—will gather into a flock that stays together throughout the winter. The birds help each other find food and watch for predators, and at night they roost together for warmth in tree cavities or in protected pockets in evergreen boughs. Flocks generally break up into pairs for the summer.

Three chickadees species are common to Alaska. The black-capped chickadee *(Parus atricapillus)* and boreal chickadee *(P. hudsonicus)* are found mostly in the Interior, where they prefer wooded areas and nest in holes in trees. Black-capped chickadees are easy to recognize with their dark black cap and chin, white cheeks, and gray back. Boreal chickadees have less pronounced markings, with a brownish cap, grayish cheeks, and reddish brown back.

Alaska's third species, the chestnut-backed chickadee *(P. rufescens)*, occurs mostly in Southeast and Southcentral. This little bird looks like a chestnut-colored version of the black-capped chickadee, and also prefers woodlands.

CORMORANT Tall, sleek, and black—cormorants are a familiar sight on ferry piers and rocks. Standing spread-winged, they pose like thunderbirds, drying their feathers after diving underwater to catch a fish.

These large, long-necked waterbirds are exceptional divers known to plunge to depths of 120 feet in search of fish to eat. Three species are common in Alaska; all are black and about 2½ feet tall. The double-crested cormorant *(Phalacrocorax auritus)* has a yellow-orange throat and is found along lakes and rivers as well as around inshore marine waters—the only cormorant to frequent freshwater.

The pelagic *(P. pelagicus)* and red-faced *(P. urile)* cormorants both have red throat and face patches during the breeding season and are usually found around inshore marine waters. Pelagic cormorants are the species most commonly found in Southeast; all three species occur in Southcentral and Southwestern Alaska.

Pelagic cormorant

Even though cormorants are considered waterbirds, their feathers are only lightly oiled. This allows them to be less buoyant so they can dive deeper, but requires them to dry their feathers after a swim. Cormorants also have heavier, denser bones than most other birds and can squeeze the air from their plumage, two factors that contribute to the cormorant's diving ability.

Except for occasional grunting on the nest, cormorants don't make a sound. Tlingit people tell this legend explaining the cormorant's silence: As usual, Raven was hungry. So he tricked some people into leaving their village in order to raid the houses. He filled a stolen canoe with goods and took Cormorant as a slave to paddle. After Raven had eaten all the food he became hungry again, and ordered Cormorant to catch him some fish. Doing as he was told, Cormorant filled the canoe with halibut.

Raven had earlier bragged about his own fishing prowess and now he worried that if Cormorant told the truth, Raven's laziness would be exposed and he would be disgraced.

"What is that on your tongue?" he suddenly asked Cormorant. When Cormorant put out his tongue to look, Raven yanked it out. To this day, Cormorant stares out to sea, unable to tell his story.

COYOTE In Alaska, wolves are still top dog. Coyotes (*Canis latrans*) are relative newcomers, having first shown up in the state shortly after the turn of the twentieth century. From Southeast Alaska—their apparent first stop in the state—coyotes expanded their range north through the upper Tanana Valley. "Song dog" populations were at their peak around 1940, then began a general decline. Today, most of Alaska's coyotes live on the Kenai Peninsula and in the Matanuska–Susitna Valleys and Copper River valley.

You still have a better chance of seeing wolves in Alaska than coyotes. The presence of wolves is a limiting factor for coyote populations; where wolves are abundant, song dogs make themselves scarce. The elimination of wolves from their traditional ranges in the Lower 48 have likely contributed to the expansion of coyote populations there.

CURLEW In all the world, western Alaska is the only known nesting area of the uncommon bristle-thighed curlew. *Numenius tahitiensis* has an unusually small range for a shorebird, summering in Alaska and wintering in Hawaii and on other central Pacific islands.

Very little is known about the brownish bird, whose Alaskan breeding area in the Yukon-Kuskokwim Delta wasn't discovered by biologists until the late 1940s. Nests are simple depressions in lichens on dry, exposed ridges. Inuit people called this curlew *chiuit*, a rendition of the bird's own voice. Around August, the bristle-thighed curlew arrives back in the Pacific islands, where it prefers undisturbed sandy shorelines and secluded short-grass fields. This rare, inscrutable, foot-tall shorebird with a long, down-curving bill and buffy cinnamon rump is sometimes seen on Hawaiian golf courses.

Chiuit's slightly smaller but similar-looking cousin, the Northern curlew *(Numenius borealis)*, hasn't been seen in Alaska since 1886. Listed as endangered, but realistically near extinction, a few pairs are thought to be holding out in northwestern Canada. Northern curlews were once called "doughbirds" because of the way they fattened up before migration.

See also SHOREBIRD

DALL SHEEP If you're ever lucky enough to see two wild bighorn sheep clash horns, you'll understand in an intuitive flash the true meaning of the word "ram." Most of this horn smashing takes place during the late fall breeding season, or rut. The male protagonists rear, run a few steps on their hind legs, come down into a full charge, and—*crack*. For all its drama, the clashing is more contest than fight. Wild sheep society is rigidly hierarchical, and ramming establishes an individual's rank.

Except for a short period during the rut, males and females stay separate, rams in bachelor groups and ewes in their own bands of females and offspring. These small herds typically consist of a half dozen or so animals, but others may mingle at mineral licks or good feeding spots.

Dall sheep

Both male and female sheep have horns, but the males' are significantly larger and heavier. (Ewes don't ram.) By the age of four, a ram's horns have usually grown into a half circle, or "half curl." Full curl generally isn't reached until a ram is seven or eight. As the horns grow, each year's growth sections are marked by distinctive dark lines called annulus rings. These rings make it possible to tell a sheep's age, if you get close enough to count.

Dall sheep *(Ovis dalli)* use the most rugged terrain in the most rugged mountains of central and Northern Alaska. Ideal sheep habitat has open ridges in combination with meadows for grazing and steep terrain for escaping predators.

Dall sheep, or white sheep as they're also called, are found only in Alaska, the Yukon Territory, and northern British Columbia. They're slightly smaller than Rocky Mountain bighorn sheep *(Ovis canadensis)* and have a white, not tan, coat. Dall rams can be 3½ feet tall at the shoulder and weigh up to 160 pounds; ewes are about 20 percent smaller. Mountain goats, the other white animal roaming Alaska's high country, have goatees and shaggier coats, and their horns are black and dagger-like.

Dall sheep take their name from the scientist William Healy Dall, who first formally described them. The American zoologist came north in the late nineteenth century on behalf of the Smithsonian Institution and various federal agencies to study the territory's natural history.

See also HORNS AND ANTLERS; MOUNTAIN GOAT

DINOSAUR Alaska boasts the northernmost fossils found in the world. Dinosaur bones were first discovered here in 1961, by a geologist who was actually exploring for oil along a remote spot of the Colville River in arctic Alaska.

Following that first discovery, the fossil bones, skin imprints, teeth, and tracks of at least six different types of dinosaurs—both flesh eaters and plant eaters—have been uncovered on the North Slope of Alaska. The dinosaurs who left these bones behind were walking around about 65 million to 70 million years ago, during the very late Cretaceous period of the Mesozoic era—right before the great dinosaur extinction.

Even older than the North Slope bones are the footprints of a carnivorous dinosaur found on the Alaska Peninsula. These tracks are thought to date back about 150 million years to the Jurassic period of the Mesozoic era.

DIPPER Charcoal gray and shaped like a plump wren, the dipper is also known by its native name *anaruk kiviruk,* "old woman sunk." Not only does this bluebird-sized songbird walk underwater against strong currents, it finds something to sing about even in the dark of winter, in a melodious, wren-like voice. The name "dipper" comes from the bird's habit of bobbing up and down in a sort of short-circuited genuflection.

Year-round residents of Alaska, these "water ouzels," as they are sometimes called, can be found in clear, fast-running streams throughout the state except for the Far North and some areas of Western Alaska. Their nests look like little huts woven from moss, and are built on rocks or cliffs, or sometimes behind a waterfall. If their home stream freezes, dippers find open, spring-fed areas or estuaries to occupy until spring.

The American dipper *(Cinclus mexicanus)* is the only truly

aquatic songbird in the world, and can swim underwater with strong strokes of its stubby wings. Once submerged, however, the bird prefers to walk along the bottom, grasping rocks with its toes, head bent into the current, looking for fish or aquatic insects to eat.

> Dippers are the only aquatic songbirds in the world and can swim underwater.

Although they are passerines (perching songbirds), dippers have a few physical adaptations more common among waterfowl. Their large preening gland helps them keep their feathers oiled, and a thick layer of down under the dense feathers works like an insulating dry suit.

DOLLY VARDEN The way fish historians tell it, an ichthyologist who had discovered a new species of char (a member of the Salmonidae family, which also includes salmon and trout) was pondering what to name it. While in the throes of this problem, he went to a dance, where he spent most of the evening whirling a lady in a colorful dress whose pattern reminded him of the silvery, orange-and-red polka-dotted fish. Perhaps between glasses of punch, he decided to name the fish after the fabric pattern, which had been inspired by a gaily dressed coquette named Dolly Varden in Charles Dickens's 1841 novel *Barnaby Rudge*.

Extremely adaptable, Dolly Varden *(Salvelinus malma)* are abundant in nearly all coastal waters of Alaska. They hatch out of nests, or redds, in gravel streambeds and spend three to six years in freshwater before migrating to the ocean. Unlike Pacific salmon, who spend years at sea, Dollies return to freshwater every fall to overwinter in a lake or stream. Dollies don't necessarily winter in the waters where they were born, but like salmon, when it comes time to spawn, they return to their stream of origin. Unlike salmon, Dollies may live to spawn more than once.

Dolly Varden were once thought to prey mercilessly on young salmon and salmon eggs. A bounty program established in 1921 paid up to five cents for each Dolly tail turned in. By the time the program ended in 1940, rewards had been paid on

Dolly Varden

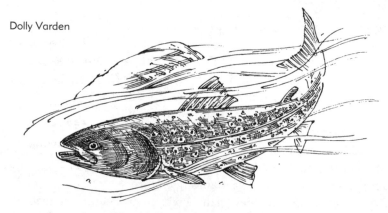

more than six million tails. As it turns out, the bounty program
was a tragic fiasco. Investigators discovered that a great percentage of the tails were actually from rainbow trout and salmon, the
very species they were trying to protect. And closer study of predation habits revealed that Dollies were eating drifting salmon
eggs that had been dug up by salmon in the act of building their
nests. So Dollies were actually providing a service to the salmon
and the ecosystem by eating debris eggs before they could
develop fungus that might infect healthy eggs. Dolly Varden also
eat freshwater snails, an intermediate host of a parasite that can
cause blindness in juvenile sockeye and coho salmon.

Although they vary widely in size, Dolly Varden tend to grow
largest in northwestern Alaska, where a good-sized fish is about
twenty inches long and weighs up to four pounds—although
nine- to twelve-pound fish have been reported. Dollies are one of
Alaska's most popular sport fish. Not only is the pink-meated fish
delicious, it is also the only member of the Salmonidae family
besides salmon readily adapted to Alaska's multitudinous small to
medium-sized coastal streams.

See also ARCTIC CHAR

DOLPHIN AND PORPOISE Five species of small
cetaceans jazz up Alaska's marine waters: three dolphins and two
porpoises.

The order Cetacea includes three groups: dolphins, porpoises, and whales. In most cases, it's pretty easy to tell when

you're looking at a whale, but distinguishing dolphin from porpoise isn't as simple—there are no absolute visual clues to who's who. Both are about the same size, can have blunt or beaked noses, and may be marked in a variety of ways.

You're most likely to encounter Alaska's two porpoises (family Phocoenidae), as they often share the protected waters of the Inside Passage with human boaters. The six-foot-long harbor porpoise *(Phocoena phocoena)* is often seen close to shore. All other porpoises or dolphins of similar size are strikingly marked, but the harbor porpoise has no fancy paint job—its darkish gray-brown back simply fades into lighter, pinkish gray sides that fade into a whitish belly. Another clue to the harbor porpoise's identity is the way it travels through the water with a sort of unhurried decorum.

In sharp contrast, the Dall porpoise *(Phocoenoides dalli)* is highly graphic and hyperactive in motion. Dalls race through boat wakes and tear across the water, splashing and dashing. The seven-foot Dalls look like little orca whales, with jet black bodies and snow white aprons.

Orca, or "killer," whales are actually the biggest member of the dolphin family (family Delphinidae), but because of their size are commonly thought of as whales. Dolphins are the largest and most diverse family within the cetacean order.

Of Alaska's three small dolphin species, you're most likely to see the Pacific white-sided species *(Lagenorhynchus obliquidens)*. These beautiful swimmers have grayish green backs, pale gray side patches, and bright white bellies. Often traveling in schools of a hundred or more, they love to ride the wakes of boats.

There is a method to this madness for surfing. Dolphins and porpoises position their bodies in such a way that the force of the wave carries them along with little physical exertion—a good way to ride out storms, as well as have some fun with tour boats.

See also WHALES

EAGLE Alaska is the land of eagle encounters—a place where casual observers can see bald eagles soaring through the air, roosting thickly in trees, standing by the road, or wading in a stream and surveying the selection of spawning salmon.

Our national symbol is far more abundant in Alaska than anywhere else in the United States, with about fifty thousand bald eagles *(Haliaeetus leucocephalus)* distributed throughout all but the northernmost and some western areas of the state. Most stay all year, although some do migrate to the Lower 48 for the winter. Of those that stay, the highest winter concentrations are found along the Chilkat River near Haines, where more than three thousand congregate in late fall and early winter to feast on spawning chum salmon—a gathering unequaled by any other eagle species anywhere else in the world.

Fish comprise the major component of a bald eagle's diet, although bald eagles will sometimes hunt waterfowl and small mammals. The opportunistic birds also commonly scavenge carrion, which is why they are often seen standing by roadkills.

Bald eagles begin life covered in mottled brown plumage and don't molt into the distinctive white heads and tails until they're around four or five years old—about the same time they become sexually mature. Known to live twenty and more years, bald eagles establish long-term pair bonds and, when possible, return to the same nest year after year, making repairs if necessary. Nests may be taken over by new occupants if something happens to the old pair, so some eagle nests might be decades old.

Eagles see you long before you see them, but they're easy to spot once you develop the right "search images." Look for white dots near the tops of large dead trees or close to the trunks of live conifers. Look also in the sky for a large, graceful bird doing more gliding than flapping; with wingspans of up to eight feet, eagles are built to soar.

Bald eagle

Before European settlement, bald eagles were common along every major river and lakeshore in the continental United

States. For a while, it seemed as though Alaska might be the repository of yet another species extirpated from the Lower 48, but recovery programs are doing very well and it looks like Alaska's bald eagles won't be alone in the world.

The slightly smaller golden eagle *(Aquila chrysaetos)* also lives in Alaska, although in fewer numbers than the bald. Steller's sea eagle *(Haliaeetus pelagicus)* is occasionally seen in the Southeast and Southwestern parts of the state, and white-tailed eagles *(H. albicilla)* sometimes show up in the Aleutian Islands.

EIDER DUCK Outfitted in the finest down underwear this side of Siberia, eiders are well suited for life as one of the most northerly of all sea ducks. Like all sea ducks, eiders basically come ashore only to nest and molt; the rest of their lives are spent on the open water.

All four eider species nest in Alaska, many remaining in the state's coastal waters for the winter. During migrations to and from nesting, molting, and wintering areas, huge numbers fly predictably over points of land known as "eider passes." More than a million fly west past Point Barrow in the late summer, and seventy-five thousand eiders have been reported over the Yukon Delta on a single day in May.

Drakes, or males, of all four species are a boldly patterned black and white; king eiders *(Somateria spectabilis)* and spectacled eiders *(S. fischeri)* also have bright markings of green and orange. All hens are brown to rusty, some with black bars or mottling.

The common eider *(S. mollisima)* is the largest wild duck in the Northern Hemisphere, weighing up to six pounds. This is the duck from which most eiderdown comes. Nesting female eiders, like many other birds, pluck the down from "brood patches" on their underside. The feathers insulate the ground nest, and the bare spot on the female allows her to transfer her body heat to the incubating eggs.

Northern Native peoples traditionally collected the down from nests and also made bird-skin parkas from eiders' feathered pelts. Today, down for coats and comforters is still collected by hand from the nests of wild eiders, in a careful way that does not affect the nesting success of the ducks. Collectors must visit forty nests to gather one pound of eiderdown—prized above the down of all other waterfowl for its insulating ability and strength. Common eider populations are in decent shape, having increased and stabilized since a decline in the 1950s to 1990s.

In contrast, spectacled eider populations are declining by as much as 90 percent in some flocks. As a result, this eider was placed on the federal list of threatened species in 1992. Spectacled eiders have eluded scientific scrutiny better than perhaps any other North American waterfowl. Most of the world's population is known to nest in the Yukon Delta, but where they spent the winter was a great mystery until the winter of 1994, when biologists discovered large numbers of spectacled eiders drifting in ice-free areas of the Bering Sea.

ELK In 1929, after an absence of about a million years, eight elk from the Olympic Peninsula of Washington State were turned loose on Afognak Island, just north of Kodiak Island. Fossil evidence shows that a subspecies of elk was present in Interior Alaska in the Pleistocene, but all elk in the Great Land today are descendants of those eight repatriates.

> **The current Alaskan elk population grew from eight individuals introduced in 1929.**

By 1965, the eight had become about fourteen hundred, but severe winters in the late 1960s and early 1970s took a heavy toll. Weather moderated over the next two decades, and elk herds are once again building; the current population numbers about one thousand. In 1986, fifty elk were moved from Afognak to Etolin Island near Petersburg in Southeast Alaska. Previous relocations to Southeast were unsuccessful, but the latest transplants appear to be taking.

The original eight Olympic Peninsula elk were of the Roosevelt subspecies *(Cervus elaphus roosevelti)*. Roosevelt elk are larger and darker than the more familiar and more numerous Rocky Mountain elk *(C. elaphus nelsoni)*, and they evolved specifically for living in a heavily timbered coastal environment. Bull elk on Afognak Island can weigh up to thirteen hundred pounds.

Only bull elk have antlers, which they shed and regrow every year. Alaskan bulls distinguish themselves with the unique tendency to form three "points" at the end of each antler—an antler that may already have three or more points off the main branch. And only the bulls make the spine-tingling mating call, or "bugle"—a high-pitched wail that announces fall has come to a wild place.

See also HORNS AND ANTLERS

EULACHON Ancient Greeks had olives, ancient Alaskans had eulachon—a species of smelt so oily that the fish could be fitted with a wick and used as a candle. Candlefish, as they're also called, were a major source of food, oil, and trade goods for many groups of Alaska Natives. Historical reference is made to well-traveled *kleena,* or "grease trails"—trading routes between Southeast Alaska and British Columbia. The original "Indian ice cream" was made from eulachon oil whipped with soapberries.

Hooligan, the other common name for this slim, silvery blue, eight-inch fish, is a variation on the pronunciation of eulachon (pronounced YOU-la-kon), a word from the Chinook Indians' trading jargon. The fish are found in most major river systems from Southeast west to Cook Inlet and also occur in lesser numbers west to the Aleutian Islands and Pribilof Islands in the Bering Sea.

Eulachon lay their eggs in the lower reaches of rivers and streams, but upon hatching, the young fish drift immediately out into the ocean, spending no significant time in freshwater. While at sea, hooligan are a major source of food for larger fish and marine mammals such as seals, sea lions, and whales. After three to four years, the smelt return to freshwater in huge schools to spawn and die. Even today, great excitement accompanies a hooligan run; people charge down to the water with small nets to dip into the silvery cloud of *Thaleichtys* ("plentiful fish") *pacificus* streaming upriver.

FALCON Two of North America's most alluring birds of prey can be found in Alaska: the peregrine falcon *(Falco peregrinus)* and the gyrfalcon *(F. rusticolus)*.

The crow-sized peregrine, which breeds throughout Alaska, is known for the 180-mile-per-hour hunting dives, or "stoops," it makes to knock flying prey from the air. Also known as duck hawks, peregrines prefer to chase waterfowl and shorebirds, but will also hunt ptarmigan and even sneak over ocean waves to snatch floating seabirds.

Peregrine falcons were listed as an endangered species in 1970, but thanks to aggressive conservation measures, the bird became one of our great wildlife success stories. The arctic peregrine *(F. peregrinus tundrius)* was removed from the list in 1994, and the American peregrine *(F. peregrinus anatum)* was removed in 1999. Peregrines are still protected under the Convention on International Trade in Endangered Species (CITES)

These avian travelers have the most extensive worldwide range of any bird. Before it was the name of a falcon, the word peregrine meant "having a tendency to wander." In the winter, solo peregrines wander as far south as Tierra del Fuego. Birds radio-tagged on the Yukon River have been tracked to such diverse winter destinations as Honduras and the Florida Everglades.

Gyrfalcons, on the other hand, stay north all year. Purely creatures of high latitudes, gyrfalcons are the largest and most elusive of all northern falcons. About the size of the familiar red-tailed hawk, gyrfalcons can be almost pure white to nearly black. Ptarmigan are the major prey, but gyrs also hunt other grouse, seabirds, shorebirds, waterfowl, ground squirrels, voles, and lemmings.

In most raptor species, females are noticeably larger than males, and this is especially true for the female gyrfalcon, who might be 30 to 40 percent heavier than her mate.

Raptors—birds of prey—are commonly divided into three groups. Hawks and eagles comprise the first group: stocky birds with broad wings and wide, rounded tails that are often seen soaring. Birds of the second group are called accipiters and include the Cooper's hawk and goshawk; accipiters have shorter, rounded wings and longish tails, and fly with several rapid wing beats followed by a short glide. Falcons, including kestrels and merlins, make up the third group. Falcons have pointed wings and long tails, and fly with short, rapid wing beats.

FLYING SQUIRREL A lot goes on in the woods between dusk and dawn, especially in the busy nightlife of the northern flying squirrel *(Glaucomys sabrinus)*. There are fungi to be foraged and owls to be eluded, dens to be relocated and rearranged.

Because they're strictly nocturnal, we rarely see these lovely little squirrels, even though they're fairly common woodland creatures. But we can listen for the telltale chirps and thumps of flying squirrels moving around in the dark.

Northern flying squirrels can be found from Southeast into the Interior—the farthest north and west this species can be found. Smaller than the gray squirrels common to suburban yards and parks, northern flying squirrels have huge eyes and silky, cinnamon brown fur. They nest in old woodpecker holes or in chambers excavated in witches'broom, and they also make ball-like nests of moss, lichen, twigs, and leaves, lined with shredded bark and more lichen.

Northern flying squirrel

Restless creatures that they are, one squirrel might use up to twenty different dens in a year. Flying squirrels don't hibernate, although in especially cold weather they may huddle together in groups in a state of light, transitory hibernation known as torpor.

Underground mushrooms are the flying squirrel's favorite food. Squirrels root out the aromatic fungal fruits and eat them, subsequently dispersing the spores in their droppings. Because the mushrooms are an important and beneficial mycorrhizal fungus, flying squirrels are considered significant components of ecosystem health and forest regeneration.

Flying squirrels don't really fly, but they're stupendous gliders. By adjusting its legs, a flying squirrel controls the shape and angle of the patagium, or gliding skin, stretched along each side of its body from wrist to ankle. On takeoff, the squirrel holds out its legs to form a large gliding surface. On the downward gliding approach to a tree-trunk landing, it raises its tail to engineer an upward swoosh and accompanying stall, slowing down to grab the tree. Almost instantaneously, the nimble rodent runs around to the other side of the trunk to foil any hungry owl that may be following too closely.

See also MUSHROOM

GEESE   Each summer about ten million swans, geese, and ducks find their nesting sites in grassy tundra meadows, on the lakeshores, along the coast, and tucked into marshes and wetlands of Alaska's wilderness. Come fall, many species migrate to the Lower 48 and points as far south as Panama. While most leave, some waterfowl species stay for the winter. Two of Alaska's year-round residents are the emperor goose and the Vancouver Canada Goose.

Canada Goose   Canada geese are icons of the Northland. They announce spring to the winter weary, and a few months later their honking sends the first fall shivers down many an Alaskan back. Alaska is rich in Canada geese—it is the summer home to five subspecies and year-round residence of a sixth. The six geese vary in size from four to fourteen pounds, but all have the distinctive Canada goose look: black head and neck, white chin strap, brown body, white rump, and black legs and feet.

Alaska's largest Canada goose and resident honker is the Vancouver subspecies (*Branta canadensis fulva*). Weighing up to fourteen pounds, Vancouver Canada geese are essentially non-migratory and remain in their Southeast Alaska home range all year. Because they must adapt their eating habits to fit the season,

Vancouvers are omnivorous, supplementing a diet of grasses and rootstock with clams, salmon eggs, and dead salmon. Although nearly every other goose species—Canadian or not—nests on the ground in marshy or grassy areas, Vancouver geese nest in old-growth forests, building nests among the dense shrubs and even occasionally high in a tree. Flightless goslings somehow manage to get down unharmed.

> Vancouver Canada geese are the only species of goose that nest in old-growth forests.

As with most species of goose, Canada geese are very social. Mates form long-term pair bonds, and the parents and their four to five offspring stay together for at least a year, migrating as a family unit. In Canada goose flocks, families enjoy the highest status, followed by mated pairs, then singles. Try to spot the different groups in the next flock you see.

Although Vancouver Canada geese don't range much farther north than Southeast Alaska, one or more of the other five subspecies are found in every other region all the way to the North Slope. The other subspecies from largest to smallest are dusky Canada goose *(B. c. occidentalis)*, lesser Canada goose *(B. c. parvipes)*, Taverner's Canada goose *(B. c. taverneri)*, Aleutian Canada goose *(B. c. leucopareia)*, and cackling Canada goose *(B. c. minima)*.

The small Aleutian Canada goose is the rarest of all the Canada subspecies. Predation by foxes introduced to the Aleutian Islands for fox farming decimated the Aleutian Canada goose population, which numbered fewer than eight hundred by the late 1960s, but today, seven thousand geese can attest to the effectiveness of recovery programs.

Emperor Goose Virtually the entire world's population of emperor geese—the rarest and arguably most beautiful geese in all of North America—are year-round residents of Alaska.

About the size of a large mallard duck, the emperor goose has a brilliant white head, pink beak, and black throat. The white head feathers continue down the back of the goose's neck, but the front of its neck and rest of its body are covered with blue-gray feathers, each of which is edged by a band of black tipped with white. A white tail and orange feet put the finishing touches on this striking goose.

Emperor geese *(Chen canagica)* nest in the Yukon-Kuskokwim Delta area of Western Alaska. Seldom far from salt water, emperors spend the winter along beaches of Kodiak Island and the Aleutians. The geese eat certain seaweeds, an occasional shellfish, and eelgrass, a member of the pondweed family that grows in the shallow waters of protected bays or river deltas. Although many species of ducks winter in Alaska, the emperor and a subspecies of Canada goose are the only two geese that winter in the state.

From 1964 to 1986, emperor goose populations fell by more than two-thirds. The decline has been attributed to heavy subsistence harvest of nesting adults and eggs, and low first-year survival of young. Since conservation programs were instituted in the mid-1980s, numbers have been rebuilding. About 70,000 emperor geese breed today on the Yukon-Kuskokwim Delta, about half the number existent in1964

Emperor geese are very gregarious and appear to form long-term pair bonds; monogamy and fidelity to family are common to most goose species.

GRAYLING

Alaska has provided safe haven for many species that have lost—or almost lost—their claw-, toe-, and talon-holds in the Lower 48. Grizzly bears, wolves, and bald eagles live on in the Northland, and now Alaska is providing a fin-hold for one more animal nearly lost to the rest of the United States: the arctic grayling. Once common as far south as Montana and Michigan, *Thymallus arcticus* has all but disappeared in the Lower 48 because of habitat loss, competition from introduced species, and overfishing.

Even here, biologists worry about grayling populations in rivers close to roads and population centers, but in the

Male grayling display their showy dorsal fin during courtship and use it to enfold the female while spawning.

free-flowing streams and lakes of Alaska's bush, arctic grayling thrive. The fish are widely distributed throughout the state from the Alaska Range north.

Arctic grayling are an iridescent gray and have long, banner-like, flat-topped dorsal (back) fins dotted with shining spots of purple or red. Such a showy fin must have some function, and indeed it does. Male grayling display the fin while courting, and, if successful, fold the fin over the female's back while the two spawn. Thus enwrapped, they arch their backs, shudder, and release eggs and milt into a small depression in the streambed formed by their vibrations.

Grayling can be very territorial, with the larger fish controlling the heads of pools where the most drifting insects can be eaten. Territories are claimed and defended through an intricate, ritualistic encounter that has the two grayling drifting back and forth, nearly touching, through the territory in dispute.

Because grayling overwinter in frigid water under ice, little food is available to them during the cold months. They prepare by eating voraciously all summer long, feeding on the adults and larvae of such insects as caddis flies, mayflies, and stone flies, and also sometimes eating salmon eggs and young. The fiercely hungry fish have even been known to eat an occasional small rodent. The biggest grayling recorded in Alaska weighed almost five pounds and was taken from the Bristol Bay area; grayling over three pounds are considered trophy catches.

GROUSE
Alaska's grouse are hardy, if perhaps not too brainy. They might not always be able to figure out how to get out of your path, but they do know how to survive a northern winter. Grouse escape howling storms by hunkering down in the snow, and elude starvation by subsisting on tough spruce needles. Special bacteria in their gut help the hen-like birds digest winter roughage until they can return to the more palatable spring fare of berries, insects, plants, and seeds.

What grouse lack in intellect, they make up for in élan: male grouse are famous for their theatrical courtship displays. Depending upon the species, they dance, hoot, flutter bomb, feather fluff, strut, drum, and flash naked skin patches that turn from yellow to red to yellow to red. Four forest or upland grouse species strut their stuff here (ptarmigan are arctic or alpine grouse).

The spruce grouse *(Canachites canadensis)* is widespread throughout Alaska's forests but is most common around Bristol Bay, on the Kenai Peninsula, and in areas of the Kuskokwim, Yukon, and Tanana river valleys. This grouse prefers spruce-birch forests with lush understory plants.

Sharp-tailed grouse *(Pediocetes phasianellus)* are found in the brushy grasslands and open woodlands of the Interior. Wildfires are important to sharp-tails because fires keep their preferred habitats open and encourage the healthy growth of plant foods.

Ruffed grouse *(Bonasa umbellus)* live in Interior woodlands and in a few river drainages of Southeast. Courting cocks "drum" with their wings; the sound is made by the grouse's cupped wings clapping the air.

The blue grouse *(Dendragapus obscurus)* is found only in Southeast, where it most commonly lives in dense forests of Sitka spruce and hemlock. Blues are also known as "hooters" for their tooting mating calls, often made while perched up in an ever-green tree. The hooting sounds like air blowing across the top of a pop bottle and is made with air sacs on either side of the grouse's neck.

See also PTARMIGAN

GULL Every Alaskan cannery has its own gleaming gray, crying cloud. Every laden fishing vessel has one, every tourist ship, and every coastal town dump. Alaska has more than half a dozen species of gulls. Among the most visible are the two largest: the glaucous *(Larus hyperboreus)* and glaucous-winged *(L. glaucescens)* gulls. Both have white heads, gray backs and wings ("glaucous" means pale bluish gray or bluish white), and pink legs. In the winter their heads become heavily flecked with gray. Both will catch fish to eat but prefer to scavenge for carrion in tidal areas. Glaucous-winged gulls can be a little too proactive in their scavenging; Alaskan biologist Robert Armstrong has seen aggressive gulls wade among spawning salmon, punching female salmon in the belly with their beaks to get them to expel eggs, then dashing to the salmons' vent to catch and eat the fresh eggs.

Populations of these two gulls have been growing rapidly, paralleling domestic and industrial development along Alaska's coast. Large gulls have few natural predators—most mortality comes from cannibalism and fights with their own kind over territory.

But not all gulls are jostling opportunists. Herring gulls *(Larus argentatus)* and mew gulls *(L. canus)* travel into the Interior, where they nest on the ground near lakes, ponds, and rivers. Largely because these gulls are fishers more than scavengers, their numbers are not exploding. Adult herring and mew gulls have white heads, gray backs, and black wing tips. Like glaucous gulls, some herring and mew gulls stay in south coastal or Southeast Alaska waters for the winter; others migrate as far south as Mexico.

> Some herring gulls and mew gulls stay in southcoastal or Southeast Alaska in winter.

In most gull species, juveniles—which are as large as adults—are brownish birds streaked with white or gray or black. Parents of many gull species feed their young regurgitated meals, and the dots of color on the tips of some adults' beaks are targets that youngsters peck to solicit feeding.

See also SEABIRDS

HALIBUT

"Wandering eye" is more than a figure of speech when it comes to halibut.

The halibut *(Hippoglossus stenolepis)* begins life with one eye on each side of its body, but during its first few months of life, when the fish is only about an inch long, the left eye migrates over the top of the fish's head until it's next to the right eye. By this time, the maturing halibut is swimming on its side, as it will for the remainder of its long life.

The eyes settle on the halibut's upper side, which is colored a deep brownish green, mottled with light hues and dots like a

Pacific halibut

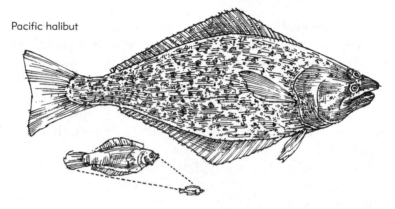

partly cloudy, partly starry night sky. Underneath, the halibut is completely white. This camouflaging coloration helps the halibut evade predators from above, such as bigger fish and marine mammals, and sneak up on prey below, including crabs, cod, pollock, and shrimp. The huge flatfish will lie in wait for a meal, sometimes buried in the sea floor up to their eyeballs, but halibut are strong swimmers and will also pursue their prey.

Most juvenile Pacific halibut spend five to seven years in relatively shallow waters of the Bering Sea known as nursery grounds. Many go on to spend their adolescence, up to about age ten, migrating in a clockwise direction around the Gulf of Alaska before dispersing more widely throughout Alaskan waters. Males become sexually mature at seven or eight years, females at eight to twelve. The oldest known female was forty-two years old; the oldest male, twenty-seven. Depending on her size, a female halibut will lay 2 million to 3 million eggs each year. Halibut are the largest of all flatfish; the largest halibut caught in Alaskan waters since record keeping began was a 495-pound barn door taken near Petersburg.

Long before there were record books or metal hooks, Alaska Native peoples relied on halibut, which they dried and smoked for winter use. Halibut hooks—some the size of a human hand—were fashioned from wood and other materials and were often decorated with carvings for good luck.

A European form of halibut gave the fish its name: from the Middle English *haly,* "holy," and *butte,* "flatfish," meaning "the flatfish to be eaten on holy days."

HORNS AND ANTLERS It's not so hard to remember: the Bovidae family (cows, sheep, goats, and bison) has horns and the Cervidae family (moose, caribou, deer, and elk) has antlers.

Horns are slow growing and permanent—if you cut one off it will never grow back. Both male and female bovids have horns, which are made from keratin, the same protein found in hair, fingernails, hooves, claws, feathers, and scales.

Antlers, on the other hand, fall off and grow back every year. In most cases only males have antlers, but caribou and reindeer are exceptions; those two are the only cervids whose males and females both have antlers, although the male's are usually larger.

While in the growing stage, antlers are covered with fuzzy skin, called velvet, which carries blood to the developing bone-like structure. When the antlers are fully formed and hardened, the animal rubs off the velvet, polishing its new antlers in the process.

Bull caribou shed their antlers after the mating season in late fall or early winter; cows shed theirs after calving in the spring. Growth begins again in the spring. The number of "points," or branches, on an antler says more about an animal's general health and availability of high-quality food than it says about age.

Both horns and antlers are used more often to beat out rival males—or to simply show off—than they are for defense against predators. When animals of both families are really mad or want to protect themselves from wolves, bears, and other threats, they lash out with their hooves.

HUMAN SETTLEMENT Humans are an important component of Alaska's natural history—after all, they've been in the region for tens of thousands of years. What was it like for those first people, camping on the upper Yukon River thirty thousand years ago? Did they hunt the woolly mammoth and saber-toothed tiger?

Although we have little information about these earliest of human residents, they were probably wandering hunters and gatherers migrating through this land from Asia via the now-vanished Bering Land Bridge, or Beringia, a low-lying plain that once connected the continents of Asia and America.

The campers on the upper Yukon River, ancestors of today's Athabascan people, traveled an inland route, hunting land animals as they went. Groups of these travelers continued south, following the retreating ice, perhaps forebears of American Native Americans in the Southwest. Other migrants to cross Beringia followed the shores, developing a coastal way of life, becoming the ancestors of the Inupiaq, Yupik and Aleut peoples. A number of distinct Native groups arose in Alaska, each with its own unique culture and language, derived from very different living environments.

The first humans in Alaska were probably migrating from Asia via the Bering Land Bridge.

Aleuts traditionally lived on the Alaska Peninsula and on islands of the Aleutian Chain, where they fished and hunted land and marine mammals for food, furs, and other uses. Evidence indicates that Aleuts have lived continuously in the Aleutians for more than eight thousand years. When Danish sea captain Vitus Bering arrived in the Aleutians in 1741, he found all habitable islands occupied. Disease, alcohol, and firearms brought by the Europeans devastated the Aleut population. Aleuts still live in the Aleutians and on the Alaska Peninsula, where many fish commercially. Only a few traditional Aleut settlements remain, however.

Alaska's arctic and northwestern coastal people fall into two main groups. The northern Inupiaq traditionally lived in Arctic Alaska and on the Seward Peninsula, while the Yupik people lived in Western Alaska from about Norton Sound to Bristol Bay. Whales, seals, polar bears, and walrus were crucial to their survival and central to their culture. A third, smaller group, the Cup'ik, also lived along the southwestern coast.

The Athabascan people roamed Interior Alaska, moving from one subsistence camp to another, following game animals and fish runs. Life was harsh, and Athabascan groups experienced frequent famine. Based on certain language and other characteristics, Athabascans are thought to be related to the Apache and Navajo peoples of the American Southwest. Today many Athabascans still make their home in Interior bush towns and villages, such as Fort Yukon and Koyukuk.

The Pacific Northwest Coast people of Southeast Alaska have cultural and language links with groups in Canada and south into Washington State. The Tlingit, Haida, Tsimshian, and Eyak people are all of the totem culture, recording their clans' history through carved mythic creatures. The Tlingit arrived before European contact. The Haida came from Canada to Alaska in the eighteenth century; the Tsimshian followed in 1887.

Southeast's plentiful seafood, deer, and other natural resources, along with its moderate weather, allowed the Native peoples to create permanent settlements and devote time to developing a rich culture full of art and ceremony.

The migration of Europeans to Alaska was sparked in 1741, when Bering's expedition arrived in the Aleutians. Bering, who was traveling under the sponsorship of Peter the Great of Russia, carried back news of abundant sea otters, drawing an influx of fur-hungry Russian and Canadian traders. Russia claimed the Alaska territory, establishing permanant Russian settlements at Three Saints Bay on Kodiak Island in 1784 and at Old Sitka in 1799. When the fur trade declined, Russia sold its New World outpost to the United States in 1867 for $7.2 million.

Five years later, in 1872, gold was discovered at Sitka, luring a new wave of fortune-seekers north for a series of gold strikes that lasted about thirty years. In 1940 another wave of people migrated north, this time brought by the United States government to two new military bases during World War II. Alaska's population in 1940 was about evenly distributed between Native (32,458) and non-Native (40,000) residents.

In addition to the military, opportunities in mining, fishing, logging, and oil—along with hunting, fishing, and the allure of a frontier lifestyle—have continued to bring newcomers to this wilderness. Today Alaska's 698,000 people are clustered primarily in the cities, especially Anchorage, although many Natives and non-Natives still live subsistence lifestyles in the bush. Despite humans' increased presence and activity, the natural landscape has so far remained essentially intact by virtue of Alaska's sheer size and inaccessibility.

See also BERINGIA

ICEWORM

Their bellies were a bilious blue, their eyes a bulbous red,
Their backs were gray, and gross were they, and hideous
of head.
And when with gusto and a fork the barman speared
one out,
It must have gone four inches from its tail-tip to its snout.

—Robert Service

They're not blue of belly, hideous of head, or four inches long—but iceworms do actually exist. First discovered in 1887 on Muir Glacier in Glacier Bay, iceworms (*Mesenchytraeus* spp.) look like miniature earthworms and may be yellow, white, brown, or black. The inch-long annelids (segmented invertebrates such as earthworms) live in the top few feet of glaciers in channels of water between ice crystals.

Iceworms can't live at temperatures much below freezing or much above 40°F. Even in winter, many Alaskan glaciers hover around a stable 32°F, except perhaps at the very surface—so even in the Alaska Range, glaciers might contain water in the liquid state year-round.

Snow buntings and other birds (and, who knows, maybe a few barmen) eat iceworms when the nocturnal creatures creep to the glacier's surface at dusk to feed on pollen and algae.

See also GLACIER

KING CRAB Imagine living under six hundred feet of water and not being able to swim. During their annual migration from deep to shallower water, king crab walk up to a mile a day on the ocean floor, up to one hundred miles round-trip—all the while breathing easily through gills located under their shells. The late winter migration brings crab to shallower water to mate and molt their external skeletons so they can grow larger.

Alaska doesn't have an official state food, but if it did, king crab would be a prime contender. The sweet-tasting shellfish is world-renowned for its delicate flavor and firm texture. Three species of king crab are found in the state. Red king crab *(Paralithodes camtschatica)* are found in greatest numbers in Bristol Bay and the Kodiak archipelago, blue king crab *(P. platypus)* occur most abundantly around the Pribilof and St. Matthew Islands, and the golden or brown king crab *(Lithodes aequispina)* population seem to be centered in waters of the Aleutian Islands.

Crab are crustaceans, a group of invertebrates that includes shrimp, lobsters, barnacles, and sea lice, all of which have chalk-like external skeletons and jointed legs. Clams and snails belong to a different group, the mollusks, which have a more advanced shell and a muscular appendage known as a "foot."

The spiny-looking king crab has five pairs of legs. The first pair carries the pincers, the larger of which is usually on the right side. The last pair of legs are small and usually tucked up under the carapace—the "lid" part of the shell that covers the crab's back. Females use the small legs to groom their fertilized eggs,

King crab

which they brood for up to a year, carried under the tail flap. Males use their small legs to transfer sperm during mating. Young crab go through several stages over a period of several months before they finally become M&M's candy–sized replicas of the adults. There's plenty of time for growth, as king crab can live many years. The largest king crab on record—with a leg span of nearly five feet—was estimated to be between twenty and thirty years old.

Adult king crab eat worms, clams, barnacles, sea stars, sea urchins, sand dollars, other crustaceans, and occasionally even their own kind. In turn, king crab are eaten by fish, including halibut and cod, and by octopuses, sea otters, and many other marine animals. And humans, of course.

LEMMING AND VOLE These small rodents are the fast food of choice for a wide array of mammals, birds, and even large fish. (Voles sometimes take to the water to look for food or to escape terrestrial predators, only to be gobbled by a hungry trout or pike.) Also known as field mice, voles look like tubby, blunt-nosed, short-tailed, slow-moving mice. At least six species live in Alaska, in all regions and habitats except bare rocks and glaciers.

Lemmings are closely related to voles but are larger, averaging four to five inches in length; like voles they have blunt noses, short legs, and short tails. Alaska has three species of lemmings, distributed widely throughout the state and usually found in tundra or boggy habitats. Most lemmings are brown, but collared lemmings (*Dicrostonyx torquatus*) turn white in the winter—the only rodent to do so. Northern peoples use the collared lemming's white pelt to trim clothing.

Both voles and lemmings are active year-round, sustaining such predators as owls, foxes, wolves, wolverines, weasels, mink, and marten through the winter. In addition to their significant value as a prey base, these burrowing animals keep soils from becoming compacted and fertilize the earth with their droppings. Both eat primarily grasses and twigs, but some lemmings also eat snails and slugs when and where they're available.

They may be small, but voles and lemmings possess an

impressive capacity for reproduction. Female meadow voles *(Microtus pennsylvanicus)* begin propagating within a month of their own birth and produce up to three litters of six young over the course of a single summer. Fast reproduction allows populations to take advantage of a particularly good grass crop or other favorable conditions. Within only two good seasons, two individual lemmings may become a family of fifty. Their life spans are short, however—voles and lemmings live only about a year.

Lemmings don't exactly make those fabled suicide marches into the sea, but they do experience sometimes dramatic die-offs after a population explosion. As food supplies give out at the peak of the population cycle, some species begin to travel in what appear to be organized columns. Thousands die crossing sea ice, lakes, or mountains.

See also SNOWY OWL

LOON In the beginning, say Siberian Eskimos, the world was covered with water until Loon dove to the bottom and brought up mud so Earth could be made. The loon is worthy of such legends: among the strongest and deepest swimmers in the bird world, loons can dive to depths of six hundred feet, where instead of mud they now look for fish and crustaceans to eat.

The Alaskan wilderness speaks in tongues through the loon's haunting laughs, wails, cries, and coos. All five of the world's loon species breed in Alaska—the privacy-seeking birds nest on remote inland lakes, ponds, and rivers, usually locating their ground nests right next to the water. Parents are attentive and, while swimming, often carry the babies on their backs to keep the young ones warm and dry. While most individuals of the other species migrate to warmer climes in the fall, Pacific loons are commonly seen in winter waters of Southeast and Southcentral Alaska.

Because their legs are set so far back on their bodies—a boon for swimming—loons are awkward on land. The word loon

> The loon can dive to six hundred feet, where it looks for fish and crustaceans to eat.

derives from the Shetland Island word *loom,* meaning "lame." Only the mallard-sized red-throated loon can become airborne from land—the other species, all larger, must take off from the water with long, running starts.

Loons have heavier bones than most birds, allowing them to overcome buoyancy. They can also squeeze out all the air from under their feathers and deflate their lungs to further facilitate diving. Because their specific gravity is close to that of water, they can sink straight down like submarines, with nary a ripple.

With sharply pointed bills and head feathers so fine they almost look like kid leather, loons cut a very elegant figure in the water. The common loon *(Gavia immer)* is the black and white loon usually pictured on American coffee mugs and greeting cards. But the red-throated loon *(G. stellata),* with its red throat, gray head, and brown back, is the most widely distributed and probably most numerous loon in Alaska. (It is also the loon that figures frequently in Eskimo folklore.) Alaska's other species— the world's other species—are the arctic *(G. arctica),* Pacific *(G. pacifica),* and yellow-billed *(G. adamsii)* loons.

LYNX   Quiet as winter, hidden as a new moon, lynx *(Lynx canadensis)* aren't often seen by the casual observer, but they're here, spread throughout the coniferous forests and woodlands in every region of Alaska. The only wildcat in the state, lynx have thick buffy gray fur with subtle mottling and a black-tipped tail. Lynx are similar to Lower 48 bobcats, but have longer legs and long tufts of fur on their ears. Broad, heavily furred paws help the reclusive, twenty- to forty-pound cats travel quickly and silently across deep snow as they track their major prey, the snowshoe hare.

Snowshoe hare populations build and crash on about an

Lynx

eight- to eleven-year cycle, a phenomenon that directly affects lynx populations. When hare numbers are high, a large percentage of one-year-old lynx will breed and have kittens; when hare numbers are down, few yearlings reproduce. When the hare cycle declines in a certain area, lynx relocate. One radio-collared cat is known to have traveled four hundred miles in search of better hunting. In the absence of hares, lynx turn to voles, lemmings, ptarmigan, grouse, squirrels, and occasionally even caribou, Dall sheep, and foxes.

Lynx hunt mainly on the ground. Although they don't climb trees to catch tree squirrels or other small game, they are nevertheless adept at climbing, and often retreat into a tree to escape such predators as wolves or humans. Strictly carnivorous, lynx—like all wildcats—come equipped with carnassials: four large, pointed molars that, instead of meeting to crush and grind, scissor past each other like blades to cut meat.

See also SNOWSHOE HARE

MARBLED MURRELET In 1974, an amazing secret was discovered about these little seabirds: they nest in trees—sometimes as far as fifty miles from salt water. From the Aleutians to Prince William Sound, marbled murrelets nest on the ground like other seabirds, but from Prince William Sound south through Southeast Alaska and down along the Pacific Northwest coast to California, marbled murrelets nest high among the branches of old-growth conifers—a habit unique among all the seabirds.

Since that first tree nest was found near Santa Cruz two decades ago, only about a dozen such nests from Alaska to California have been located. Evidence suggests, however, that more marbled murrelets nest in Alaska's Tongass National Forest than in any other place in North America.

About the size of a robin, marbled murrelets (*Brachyramphus marmoratus*) have compact, short-necked bodies, short tails, and stubby wings. In the winter they are brown with white undersides and in the spring and summer are a mottled brown.

No one knows exactly why marbled murrelets choose to nest in the forest. Parents, which are thought to mate for life, must make long daily trips to feed their one offspring, usually carrying only a single fish at a time. And when it fledges, or flies for the first time, the youngster must fly all the way to the sea or its chances of survival are grim; many potential predators are lurking if the little bird falls to the ground.

Nests are simple depressions in thick moss on broad, flat evergreen branches. Only trees 150 years or older have moss thick enough to make suitable nests. For this reason, the non-Aleutian marbled murrelets, like spotted owls, need old-growth forests to sustain their populations. The logging of old growth in the Northwest has put the marbled murrelet at risk throughout the Pacific Northwest.

> **Marbled murrelets are the only seabirds to make their nests in trees.**

Marbled murrelets are relatively abundant in Alaska, but a 2007 US Geological Survey reported 71 percent decline from the early 1990s, with the population dropping from nearly a million birds to about 271,000. If logging of old-growth forests goes unchecked, Alaska's nesting murrelets could find themselves in jeopardy. Loss of old-growth habitat isn't the only danger to the small seabirds: marbled murrelets are also known to become entangled in gill nets and are quite vulnerable to oil spills.

See also SEABIRD

MARMOT Spending the better part of their lives either sleeping or sunbathing, marmots are the couch potatoes of Alaska's rodent world. The two- to ten-pound, twenty-inch animals look like a cross between a ground squirrel and a beaver, with stocky gray to brown bodies, short legs, small ears, and long furry tails. Alaska has three species: the Alaska marmot (*Marmota broweri*), hoary marmot (*M. caligata*), and woodchuck (*M. monax*).

Largely sedentary, "whistle pigs" stay close to their home burrows, eating grasses, roots, wildflowers, and berries, and sunning themselves when the mosquitoes aren't too bad. They also take time out to whistle at the occasional passing hiker; hoary marmots and woodchucks use their vocal cords to make a loud, whistling alarm call, and also hiss, yip, growl, and squeal. Alaska marmots usually stick to a low-pitched note, warning of such predators as eagles, foxes, wolves, and bears.

Hoary marmots live primarily on high-elevation rocky slopes among boulder piles in the mountains of Interior, Southeast, and Southwestern Alaska. The Alaska marmot lives in similar habitat in the Brooks Range. Woodchucks, or groundhogs, occupy river valleys and dry lowlands in eastern parts of the Interior. ("Woodchuck" is something of a misnomer, as these animals do not "chuck wood," even though they have the teeth for it. The name derives from a Cree Indian word used to describe a number of similar-sized animals.) All marmot species have perpetually renewing incisors, which they keep in check by chewing tough materials like willow roots and by carrying rocks during burrow construction and maintenance. Marmots are more accurately known by the nickname "rock chuck."

Woodchucks and hoary marmots hibernate in the same burrows they use in summer, either alone or in small groups composed of a mother and her two to six offspring. To protect themselves from marauding winter predators such as wolves and foxes, they plug the entrance to their sleeping chamber with a mixture of dirt, vegetation, and feces.

Unlike the other two species, Alaska marmots—in their harsh Brooks Range habitat—hibernate in a special winter den, where many individuals huddle together in a large group. When the last colony member is inside, they plug the chamber, remaining there until the plug thaws in the spring. They routinely wake before the plug thaws, and most mating takes place before the animals emerge from the den. The same winter chambers can be used decade after decade. Marmots have evolved a high tolerance for oxygen depletion and carbon dioxide—a reasonable adaptation, considering they may spend two-thirds of the year sealed in their den.

MOOSE To call moose "ungainly" is to miss the point. They may not be as gracefully proportioned as deer or elk, but moose are beautifully built for life in the Northland. With the Jimmy

Moose

Durante nose, they can smell predators and potential mates; big ears keep them alerted to what's going on around them. Long legs allow easier movement through snow and keep the moose's chest out of all but the deepest drifts, and their unique, piston-like, prancing gait is perfect for moving over wet, uneven tundra and wading through the sucking muck of ponds and shallow lakes. The moose's oversized dewclaws (two small hoof-like appendages on the back of the moose's ankle) spread out like snowshoes to help the animal maneuver through mud and snow.

The largest member of the deer family, moose *(Alces alces)* are found in woodlands throughout most of Alaska and northern regions of the Lower 48, but Alaska's moose are the largest in North America. The biggest bulls can be 7 ½ feet tall at the shoulder, weigh eighteen hundred pounds, and have antlers that span over six feet.

Moose are often seen in or near ponds, marshes, and lakes from Southeast to the Arctic Slope. They wade into water up to their backs to graze on submerged aquatic plants, plunging their big heads completely underwater to grab a mouthful, then raising their heads up, water running off antlers and drooping ears, to chew contentedly. Moose are also commonly found in areas of recent wildfires where favored forage food like willows, birch, and other plants are revegetating the burn. Based on early writings, it is thought that Athabascan peoples once set intentional fires in spruce forests to make the land more attractive to moose.

Even with their great size, massive antlers, and large, heavy hooves, moose are usually not aggressive, but they will ferociously defend themselves and their offspring, even against humans. Under rare circumstances people have been attacked and killed by defensively enraged moose.

Wolves are moose's greatest natural enemies—the two have been locked in a predator-prey relationship since wolves followed moose over the Bering Land Bridge ages ago.

See also BERINGIA; HORNS AND ANTLERS

MOSQUITO There are ways to avoid Alaska's mosquitoes. Go outdoors only in the winter, for instance. Or, if you insist on being outside any other time of year, stick to glacier walking or sailing. Shopping trips in downtown Anchorage are usually mosquito-free as well.

If these mosquito-avoidance activities don't appeal to you, put on some high-powered insect repellent, a hat, and full-coverage clothes, and go have some fun, out amongst Alaska's thirty-something known species of mosquito. Don't spend too much energy picking the best time of summer to avoid the bugs—some mosquito species or other is going to be buzzing around. Female snow mosquitoes *(Aedes communis)* can be active even when snow is still on the ground. But that said, mosquitoes do seem to be least annoying in late summer and early fall.

When you're lying in your tent on a bright, early summer day, tired of the fight, know that humans are not being exclusively singled out. Caribou suffer too—those fellow warm-bloods can lose up to a pint of blood a day to the little vampires. Mosquitoes target Alaska's hordes of nesting waterfowl as well. It would help if we could wear sky camouflage, hold our breath, and not sweat, since mosquitoes are attracted to carbon dioxide, moisture, warmth, and dark, musk-ox brown sorts of colors.

In all mosquito species, only the female bites, needing blood's quality nourishment in order to lay eggs. Males hover about in ominous numbers, but drink only plant nectar. Take some satisfaction in the fact that Alaska's mosquitoes live only about a month in the final, buzzing, biting adult stage of their lives.

One of Alaska's most troublesome mosquitoes is *Aedes excrucians*—*Aedes* meaning "repugnant," *excrucians* being self-explanatory. This species breeds in almost any wet place and bites on warm, sunny afternoons when other mosquitoes are least active. Most other mosquito species prefer dawn and dusk food forays.

Each species has a unique wing-beat frequency with which it recognizes its own members, an important consideration in reproduction. As a further aid, within each species, males have a slightly higher wing-beat frequency than females. The fastest mosquitoes fly at six hundred wing beats per second. They lift off like helicopters and must keep their wings moving or they'll crash, since they're built not to soar, but to buzz-bomb and bite.

Biting is not a haphazard procedure—as evidenced by the fact that females can breathe through holes in their abdomens in order to keep their mouthparts free for sucking blood. These mouthparts have been likened to a set of "tiny surgical tools": sensing organs detect a blood-filled capillary, which is then punctured with piercing organs. Tube organs draw out blood and also pump in saliva, stimulating blood flow and possibly inhibiting coagulation.

The Great Land's mosquitoes are infuriating but not life threatening. Because of the cold climate, mosquito-borne illnesses such as malaria and yellow fever are not a danger here. And birds and fish are all the better off for the presence of these pesky prickers. Flying insects and aquatic larvae are important strands in the food web.

See also BITING FLIES

MOUNTAIN GOAT It's never easy being a kid, but imagine being a mountain goat youngster: first you have to walk and keep up with adults when you're only a few hours old and barely bigger than a snowshoe hare, and until you get bigger, you have to worry about some golden eagle trying to knock you off your ledge so it can eat you. But mother is there, rarely more than thirty feet away, always standing on your downhill side to stop you from falling.

Even in the face of cliffs and eagles, Alaska's mountain goats *(Oreamnos americanus)* are totally at home in the steepest, rockiest, most rugged and windswept mountains from Southeast to Southcentral, and into the Interior almost to Denali National Park. Goats spend most of their time on slopes akin to a stepladder. Their two-toed, rubbery-soled hooves assure surefootedness on treacherous terrain, and their relatively flat sides allow them to negotiate narrow ledges. They can't outrun predators such as wolves and bears, but they can certainly outclimb them. Predators are less of a threat to mountain goats than avalanches and ice- or snow-related falls.

Mountain goats are often confused with Dall sheep *(Ovis dalli)*, Alaska's other large, white, horned mammal. But where sheep have massive, curled horns and short, sleek coats, both billy and nanny goats have sharply pointed black horns up to ten inches long, and thick, shaggy coats. Male and female goats look very similar; both appear to be wearing knickers because of the way their coats pantaloon over their upper legs, and both have a fringe of fur rimming the chin. (The human beard style "goatee" takes its name from the goat's original fashion statement.)

> **Predators are less of a threat to mountain goats than avalanches and ice-related falls.**

Unlike bighorn rams, mountain goat billies—up to 3½ feet tall at the shoulder and weighing up to 280 pounds—do little head-to-head sparring during the mating season; their skulls and horns aren't built to withstand such ramming. Instead, billies rely more on visual displays to attract nannies. They're not above flank-to-flank combat, however, for which they're more physically prepared: the skin on a mountain goat's rump is nearly an inch thick and was once used by some Alaska Native peoples as chest armor.

The Native Alaskan ceremonial Chilkat blankets were traditionally woven from mountain goat fur. It sometimes took an
entire year and the wool of three goats to weave a single blanket.

See also DALL SHEEP; HORNS AND ANTLERS

MUSK OX

If they look like they stepped out of the last
ice age, it's because they did. Alaska's musk oxen of today are
identical to the ones that were around one hundred thousand
years ago. Why change something that works? Wrapped in six-
inch-thick underfur and a long overcoat of windproof, snowproof
guard hairs that nearly drag on the ground, musk oxen (*Ovibos
moschatus*) are tailor-made for their environment. Short legs, short
ears, and heavy bones aid in heat conservation, and lend this
three- to five-foot-tall animal the look of a sweep of brown yarn
with horns.

Thanks to their remarkable underfur, called *qiviut*, musk
oxen are never cold; even at -50°F their metabolism barely takes
notice. *Qiviut* is warmer and more durable than wool, yet softer
and more elegant than cashmere. Native people on Nunivak
Island collect naturally shed underfur from the tundra and spin
it by hand. A domestic musk ox herd is also kept in Palmer to
produce *qiviut* for a growing cottage industry of hand-knit caps,
scarves, and other bits of clothing that are as warm as down and
as light as smoke.

Musk oxen can digest plant roughage better than any other
herbivore. Although Alaska has vast open areas, most ground is
covered with low-quality forage, not high-quality grassland. The
musk ox's digestive tract can break down woody plant material
that other animals are unable to digest. This intestinal efficiency
also allows musk oxen to get by on less food, further proving
their perfect fit in the northern environment.

Both male and female musk oxen have heavily built horns
that look somewhat like a water buffalo's. Drooping down on
either side of the face from a "part" on top of the head, the
horns curl slightly up and forward on the ends. During the
breeding season, male musk oxen engage one another in very
aggressive head bashing—although the horns' lethal tips are

reserved for predators. The impact of a full-blown charge between two bulls has been likened to a car hitting a concrete wall at seventeen miles per hour. A four-inch thickness of horn on top of a three-inch-thick skull protects the bulls' brains.

Hormone-inspired clashing aside, musk oxen are gregarious animals, living together in groups of varying size. Depending upon the season and the location, herds can number from a half dozen up to seventy-five animals. The musk ox's group defense tactic is very effective against its primary natural enemy, the wolf. When a threat is first perceived, the herd bunches into a group, facing the danger. If there is only a single predator, musk oxen form a straight-line defense. In the case of multiple attackers, adults form a shoulder-to-shoulder circle—a ring of horns—with calves in the middle. Occasionally, individuals will rush out to charge the attacker.

This strategy works quite well with wolves, but was the musk ox's undoing when human predators came on the scene. Early Native hunters learned to exploit this behavior, as did the arctic explorers and whalers who followed. By the mid- to late 1800s, Alaska's last musk ox had been killed. By 1917, musk oxen survived only in remote parts of Canada and Greenland, and seemed on the verge of extinction. In 1930, thirty-four

Musk ox

musk oxen were transported from Greenland to Fairbanks to be reintroduced to their Alaska range. Five years later the survivors and their calves were released onto Nunivak Island, where the herd grew to over seven hundred animals by the late 1960s. Musk oxen from the successful herd are now being used to reintroduce the returning native to other areas of Alaska and elsewhere— including Russia's Wrangel Island. Currently, from a world population of around ninety thousand, an estimated four thousand wild musk oxen roam Alaska's northwestern area.

MUSTELIDS

Weasels, mink, and marten make up the fast-lane branch of the Mustelidae family, a group that also includes sea otters, land otters, skunks, ferrets, and wolverines. The most obvious common denominator in the family—besides long, slender, furry bodies, short legs, round ears, and anal scent glands— is an obsession with food.

Weasels are the most high-octane family member, needing to eat 40 percent or more of their body weight every day to satisfy a frenetic metabolism. Found in woodlands, brushy areas, fields, and tundra meadows, weasels occur in every region of Alaska. The least weasel (*Mustela rixosa*), smallest member of the Mustelidae family and smallest carnivore in the world, carries only about three ounces on its eight-inch frame. (Shrews, often credited with being the smallest carnivore, are considered insectivores. Shrews are, however, the smallest mammals.) Short-tailed weasels, or ermines (*M. erminea*), are slightly larger— about twelve inches long and eight ounces—but can still slip through a mouse hole in search of prey. Both species turn from brownish in summer to white in winter, but only the ermine has a black tip on its tail. Alaska Native peoples use ermine pelts to decorate clothing.

When food supplies are abundant, weasels kill more than

> **Weasels need to eat 40 percent or more of their body weight every day to satisfy their frenetic metabolism.**

they can eat at one time because hunting is what they do; their predator program is internally hard-wired. The primarily solitary animals are known to stash surplus kills in a special side room of their burrow. Mice are the preferred food, but weasels will also catch shrews, pikas, fish, insects, birds, and the occasional young snowshoe hare. This kind of schedule doesn't leave much time for rest—weasels may be active twenty or more hours a day.

Mink *(M. vison)* live near freshwater streams and ponds and saltwater beaches and marshes, where they can find their favorite food: fish and shellfish. Mink will also eat other small mammals, birds, bird eggs, frogs, insects, and just about anything else they can catch and kill. The four-pound, two-foot-long chocolate brown animals inhabit every region of Alaska. Look for the mink's five-toed tracks and small piles of scat (droppings) on logs, rocks, and trails.

Marten *(Martes americana)* can be somewhat larger than mink. The only mustelid to routinely climb trees, this widespread and abundant animal can be found in Alaska's woodland habitats from Southeast to the farthest north limit of trees in the Arctic; most, however, live in the black spruce forests and bogs of the Interior. Also called American sable, marten have beautiful pale yellow to dark brown fur. Marten are effective predators, but they are also opportunistic, supplementing their usual diet of voles, mice, and squirrels with carrion, berries, and eggs.

See also OTTERS; WOLVERINE

OTTERS River otters and sea otters share a subfamily (Lutrineae) and a carefree attitude—eat, sleep, and be merry. The two otters comprise the easygoing side of the North American Mustelidae family, whose other branch includes such Type-A members as weasels, mink, and wolverines.

River Otter At home in both inland and coastal environments, river otters, or land otters as they're also known, are found throughout most of Alaska south of the Brooks Range, wherever there's some kind of water—especially along coastlines, salmon streams, and lakes. The whiskered *Lutra canadensis* has dark brown fur, short legs with webbed hind paws, a thick neck, and a long, thick tail. Adults can grow to three or four feet long and weigh fifteen to thirty-five pounds.

With no significant predators except humans, land otters have time to goof off. Both adults and young enjoy a good game of stick toss, rock roll, hide-and-seek, tag, dunking, or wrestling. Sliding on ice or crusted snow is another favorite activity, pursued sometimes for fun, sometimes to get where they're going more efficiently. Otters can reach speeds of fifteen miles per hour by alternately running and sliding, leaving tracks that look like they were made by a small plastic toboggan.

Although they're comfortable on land, river otters are also excellent swimmers and can dive to sixty feet, staying submerged for more than four minutes. They hunt both on land and in the water, and eat snails, fish, clams, sea urchins, insects, frogs, and occasionally birds, small mammals, and, in a pinch, vegetation.

Highly social, otters congregate in varying family arrangements within their home range of a few miles. Most typical is a female with her one to six pups, with or without a male, but other groups include male and female pairs, litter mates that stay together after the mother starts her next family, and groups of bachelor males.

In Tlingit and Haida lore, Raven bestowed on Land Otter the power to "save" people lost in or near the water by turning them into half-human, half-animal beings called Land Otter Men, or *kushtakas*. Land Otter people could be benevolent, but were more usually associated with trickery and death. Children were taught to beware Land Otter People and not to venture too far into the woods or on the water—*kushtaka* territory.

Sea Otter In the marine mammal crowd, sea otters are the svelte set. Unlike whales, walruses, seals, and sea lions, sea otters have relatively little body fat. Instead of relying on blubber to keep them warm, sea otters count on their famous fur—a luxuriant, inch-thick undercoat of brown, sprinkled with silvery guard hairs. If the fur becomes dirty, oiled, or matted, it loses its air-trapping, insulating properties, allowing the otter to become soaked to the skin and leading to possible death by hypothermia (this is why sea otters are so vulnerable to oil spills). Little wonder, then, that they spend so much time grooming—scrubbing their fur with their forepaws, bite-combing their coats, and swishing clean with a watery barrel roll.

In Alaska, sea otters *(Enhydra lutris)* are found in nearshore waters along the outer coast from Southeast Alaska to Prince William Sound and the Aleutian Islands, especially in or near kelp beds. About four feet long, sea otters weigh up to eighty pounds, and have inquisitive, whiskery faces. Seals are the other similar-sized furred marine mammal you're likely to observe, although seals are at least a foot longer and much heavier. If you see a sleek head with big eyes and no ears looking at you, it's probably a seal. But if you see a furry animal floating on its back watching the world go by, it's probably a sea otter. Air trapped in the sea otter's coat works like a buoy to keep the animal afloat. When a seal is finished looking at you and wants to disappear, it simply sinks straight down below the surface. Sea otters, on the other hand, roll over and dive.

> A sea otter eats while floating on its back, using its chest as a tray.

This largest member of the Mustelidae family (which includes weasels and wolverines) is also the smallest marine mammal. Its back paws are webbed for swimming, but the sea otter's front paws have stiff fingers with retractable claws, handy for prying abalone loose from rocks or digging crabs from a rock pile. An otter can dive to depths of sixty feet in search of sea urchins, clams, or other favorite foods, and will surface with the goods. The fastidious animal eats while floating on its back, using its chest as a tray. To get at the meat in hard-shelled prey, an otter will use a rock or another clam to smash open the shells lying on its chest. Sometimes an otter will place a flat rock on its chest to use as an anvil. Sea otters have been observed carrying a favorite pounding rock under their armpits as they dive for more food in sequential foraging dives.

Clumsy on land, sea otters rarely go ashore (even seals haul out on land to rest and have their pups, but sea otters give birth

Sea otter

in the water). In stormy weather or to keep from drifting in to shore when eating, sea otters use kelp as a sort of anchor, purposefully entangling themselves in the floating (but rooted) mats of seaweed.

Although they are social animals, often congregating in pods of a few to over one thousand individuals, sea otters don't form long-term pair bonds. Mating and birthing can occur at any time of year, but in Alaska, most females bear a single pup in the spring. Whether they reproduce every year or every other year depends in part on food supplies. Otters can live up to twenty years.

Very young pups can't dive, so they spend their early life riding on their mother's chest. Bald eagles occasionally prey on newborn sea otter pups, and killer whales may take both young and adult otters, but natural predation seems to have little effect on overall numbers. Humans have been the sea otter's real problem.

Alaska's first boom wasn't a gold rush or an oil frenzy, it was the sea otter fur trade. Because it is so thick and beautiful, sea otter fur has been among the most valuable and sought-after fur in the world. Almost immediately after Vitus Bering found his way to Alaska in 1742, the fur rush began, and by the time the United States bought Alaska from the Russians in 1867, the territory's original estimated population of 150,000 sea otters had been decimated by hunting. By 1911, only about 1,500 sea otters survived. With protection, planning, and perseverance, sea otter recovery, at least in Alaska, can be considered a rousing success. Populations are growing steadily, and sea otters have reoccupied much of their historical range. Alaska now counts its sea otters in the tens of thousands.

See also MUSTELIDS

PIKA Pikas have the body of a guinea pig, the face of a rabbit, the ears of Mickey Mouse, and the voice—*eeeeep*—of an excited squeaky toy. Alaska's single pika species, the collared pika *(Ochotona collaris),* is about the size of a large chipmunk and is grayish brown with a white collar and belly. Collared pikas live in colonies around large boulders, or on rocky or talus slopes near mountain meadows in parts of Interior and Southcentral Alaska. Even though they live in colonies, each pika has its own burrow. Feeding territories may overlap, leading to squabbles—especially in the fall, when pikas are making final preparations for winter.

The pika knows how to plan ahead. In midsummer, pikas begin to collect grasses and other plants that they stack in piles to dry. Individuals protect their own piles, but have no qualms about raiding their neighbor's cache. By fall, a single pika's haystack may be two feet high and two feet across, and contain about twelve pounds of vegetation—but a *really* industrious pika can assemble a fifty-pound stack. Hay making provides essential winter food for the nonhibernating pika's survival.

Pikas and other small, grass-eating animals don't have room in their bodies for extra stomach chambers as do cows and other large herbivores. So in order to thoroughly digest all that roughage, pikas cycle food through their entire digestive tract twice in a process known as coprophagy, which basically means "dung eating." The first time through, food is excreted as soft pellets of partly digested material. Scientists believe that the second time through, more vitamins are released from the pellets and absorbed through the small intestine. The story ends with a hard pellet of pure waste.

Also called "rock rabbit" and "little chief hare," pikas used to be classified as rodents, but now share the order Lagomorpha with rabbits and hares. Lagomorphs are distinguished from other groups by having eight incisors instead of four, and—nearly unique among all animals—the male's testes and scrotum are in front of the penis.

PTARMIGAN   Instead of flying south for the winter, ptarmigan hang tough and dig in for the duration. In fact, this North Country grouse copes with severe cold by burrowing into the snow, where it may be many degrees warmer than the air temperature. And since ptarmigan molt out of brown feathers into white for the winter, they are perfectly camouflaged from marauding predators such as foxes and snowy owls.

Surprisingly, birds can be more resistant to cold than mammals: they don't have fleshy ears and tails to dissipate heat (or become frostbitten); their feathery down is an excellent insulator; and birds have higher metabolisms, so they generate more heat.

Although ptarmigan, *Lagopus* spp., don't migrate away in the winter, they are nomadic during the cold season—moving from tundra and rock slopes to more-sheltered areas, often at lower elevations. In the fall, stiff feather mats like snowshoes begin to grow on the birds' feet (*Lagopus* means "hare-foot"), and their claws grow longer to provide better traction on snow and ice.

Summer is a feast of insects, caterpillars, leaves, catkins, and flowers, but winter fare is less luscious, consisting of the buds and twigs of willows, birch, and alder. Special bacteria in a food-storage organ, or "crop," in the ptarmigan's throat help break down roughage. The crop allows ptarmigan to stuff themselves during the short days, storing food to be digested later—often throughout the night—to help maintain body temperature.

All three of the world's ptarmigan species live in Alaska. The willow ptarmigan *(Lagopus lagopus)* is the largest of the three, weighing up to 1½ pounds; in 1955 it was chosen by Alaska's schoolchildren as the official state bird. Willow ptarmigan are found in every region of the state, although they are less common in the Southeast and southern coastal areas.

The white-tailed ptarmigan *(L. leucurus)* is the only ptarmigan found south of Canada. Less common in Alaska than the other two species, this bird is found primarily in the rugged uplands of Southcentral.

Rock ptarmigan *(L. mutus)* are distributed statewide except for the west and north coasts. Said to be the most hardy of Alaska's three ptarmigan, this species prefers higher, more barren hills.

See also GROUSE

Horned puffin

PUFFIN During the spring and summer, coastal Alaska is a veritable puffin carnival. The early sailor who nicknamed these clown-faced birds "sea parrots" must have seen them in the summer—the prominent, bright yellow and red bill is a temporary breeding display. By late summer, this colorful outer shell peels off to reveal a smaller, drabber beak.

Although they spend much of their lives drifting in waters far offshore, most of North America's 5.5 million puffins come to Alaska in the spring to nest.

The plump, foot-tall birds form colonies on rocky islands and headlands from Southeast all the way up and around to the far northwest corner of the state. Tufted puffins *(Fratercula cirrhata)* outnumber horned puffins *(F. corniculata)* almost four to one. Both birds are black and have white faces during the breeding season. The horned puffin also has a white breast during the summer; the bird's Native name, *katukh-puk,* means "big white breast." Its "horn" is a fleshy, vertical black stripe above the eye.

Tufted puffins have black breasts and two feathery crests, or tufts, curling back from their heads like wisps of hair.

Puffins nest in rock crevices or in underground burrows they dig with the strong claws of their orange, webbed feet. They lay a single egg that both parents incubate. Newly hatched chicks stay in the burrow for about six weeks, attended by both parents.

Better swimmers than fliers, puffins propel themselves underwater with their wings, using their webbed feet only to maneuver.

It seems they even walk better than they fly, balancing agilely on their toes. Propelling their stocky little bodies into flight is a lot of work. Water takeoffs require a long running start and gradual ascent, which might have a bird crashing through waves before it reaches altitude. On land, puffins avoid the trouble by launching themselves off cliffs.

Puffins were an important resource for Native peoples, who used them for food and clothing. Aleuts made parkas of puffin skins.

See also SEABIRD

RAVEN According to the mythology of some Alaska Native peoples, Raven brought the daylight, hung the moon, acquired fire, and made the rivers flow. He created people—then tricked them out of their food in a variety of clever and devious ways.

Mystical powers have been attributed to the raven as far back as ancient Greece. No wonder *Corvus corax* has a reputation as the smartest bird alive. Observant scientists believe ravens engage in complex play as a way of honing life skills, and tests have shown the birds possess the ability to learn and solve problems.

At two feet from beak to tail, ravens are the largest perching songbirds.

The largest passerines (perching songbirds) in the world, ravens can be two feet long from beak to tail. They live throughout the Northern Hemisphere, and in Alaska you can go almost anywhere, almost anytime, and be in the company of this iridescent black avian intellectual. In the winter, the nonmigratory birds fluff out their feathers in deference to the cold, but otherwise seem oblivious to subzero temperatures.

Ravens, who may live into their twenties, mate for life and appear to be affectionate with each other, touching bills, vocalizing, and flying aerobatically for what looks like fun, sometimes with wing tips touching. The male feeds the female while she's incubating eggs in a nest the pair may use every year. Offspring often stay with their parents through their first winter.

Although ravens are in the songbird group, what they do seems more like talking. Raven "words" can have up to five syllables and be "spoken" with a variety of inflections. More than thirty distinct vocalizations have been identified, from the throaty, resonant *ke-dowk* to the burbling *ko-wulk-ulk-ulk*.

The northwestern crow *(Corvus caurinus)* shares Alaska with the common raven. Crows are smaller, speak in a less musical *caw*, and have a flat-edged tail. Ravens have a stout, somewhat downcurved bill, shaggy throat feathers, and a tail shaped like a flattened pyramid.

RAZOR CLAM You can't shave with a razor clam, but you can cut your fingers on the brittle shell—ask any of the thousands of recreational clammers who dig about a million Pacific razor clams *(Siliqua patula)* a year for fun and clam fritters. The thin, flattish, oval shells can be up to seven inches long.

Razor clams are found along a number of Alaska's open ocean beaches from the Bering Sea southward, living from tide line to depths of about 180 feet. Most clam digging takes place on the sandy, surf-swept beaches of the east side of Cook Inlet.

Using their own "digger," or "foot," razor clams move down through the sand quite quickly, and if left on the surface are able to completely retrench within twenty seconds. However, clams can only move vertically through the sand, so they spend their entire lives—possibly eighteen years or more—in the same spot, buried to the tips of their "necks," or "siphons," filtering plankton from the water to eat.

Spawning is triggered by rising water temperatures in the spring. Females release eggs and males release sperm at random onto wet sand or directly into the water—a strategy known as broadcast spawning. Fertilization seems almost coincidental. Larvae drift around for five to sixteen weeks, at which time their shells begin to form. Soon after, the tiny young clams settle into the substrate forevermore.

Alaska has about two hundred other kinds of clams besides razors; culinary favorites include butter clams *(Saxidomus giganteus)* and steamers, or littlenecks *(Protothaca staminea)*.

Care must be taken when digging and eating clams because paralytic shellfish poisoning (PSP) toxins are sometimes found in Alaskan waters. PSP is caused by microscopic algae, often the dinoflagellate *Alexandrium catenella.* Filter feeders like razor and other clams can take in the toxin at no harm to themselves, and it may linger in their bodies for two years. Some PSP algae have a red pigment, thus the term "red tide."

State officials run continual tests to monitor the safety of popular clam beaches. All commercial clamming is subject to stringent regulation to assure consumer safety so diners can enjoy their chowder with confidence.

REINDEER   Reindeer and caribou don't look *exactly* alike, but biologists consider reindeer to be Old World representatives, and caribou to be New World representatives, of the same species, *Rangifer tarandus.* Practiced eyes can tell the two apart: caribou are rangier, have longer legs, and are faster. Reindeer are smaller than caribou (only about 3 to 3½ feet tall at the shoulder and about two hundred pounds) and display much more variety of color, sometimes with pinto markings on their dark brown to whitish coats.

Reindeer aren't native to Alaska. In 1891, a high-profile Christian missionary named Reverend Sheldon Jackson imported sixteen Siberian reindeer to the Seward Peninsula and arranged for Lapp herders to come teach reindeer herding to the Native residents. At that time, caribou were scarce in northwestern Alaska, and whales—another traditional source of food and materials—had been nearly cleaned out by commercial whaling. Jackson thought reindeer herding would provide Native peoples with food as well as start them on the path to a cash economy through the sale of meat and hides. In the decade following the first shipment, nearly 1,300 reindeer were transported to Alaska. By 1914 Alaska's reindeer population had grown through natural reproduction to 50,000. At the peak in the early 1930s, federal records indicate over 640,000 reindeer in the state (although those numbers are now thought to be overestimated).

Despite Jackson's good intentions, Natives gained little from the project. Initially, Lapp herders and mission churches realized the greatest benefits, and in the late 1920s white entrepreneurs took over Alaska's thriving reindeer industry. In the late 1930s and early 1940s, however, reindeer populations began a serious decline due to overgrazing, predation, and disease—even while caribou populations were on the upswing. As caribou reoccupied their traditional ranges, free-roaming reindeer were assimilated into the growing herds. Because they are the same species, the two can interbreed; it isn't known what percentage of today's caribou are part reindeer.

> Reindeer are smaller than caribou and display much more variety of color.

At the same time reindeer numbers were dwindling in the late 1930s, Outside markets had collapsed in the Depression-era economy and tensions between Native and non-Native herders were escalating. In 1937, Congress passed the Reindeer Act, which stipulates that only Alaska Native people can legally own reindeer in the state.

Today, independent Native herders raise about 25,000 reindeer, most divided into about thirteen herds in the vicinity of the Seward Peninsula, where it all began. Instead of making money off meat and hides, the most valuable modern market is in the sale of antlers—a renewable resource—to Asian buyers. Antlers, which can fetch upwards of fifty dollars per pound, are ground for use in traditional medicines and tonics.

See also CARIBOU

SABLEFISH (BLACK COD)

SABLEFISH (BLACK COD) Three thousand feet under the sea, gray-black ghosts glide through the icy waters of the North Pacific. Commonly called black cod because of their dark color and loose resemblance to the cod family, sablefish aren't even related to cod. In fact, the only kin of the streamlined, rough-skinned *Anoplopoma fimbria* is the relatively rare skilfish.

Living as they do in such cold depths—typically twelve hundred to three thousand feet—sablefish are insulated with an unusually high fat content. This elevated level of oil, rich in omega-3 fatty acids, makes the three- to ten-pound fish greatly prized as food and an important commercial species in Alaska. Commercially harvested black cod are caught on hooks as far down as five hundred fathoms, or three thousand feet.

Ninety percent of Alaska's sablefish catch is exported to Japan, but black cod, sometimes called "butterfish" for its rich taste, is gaining favor on American tables. The delicate white meat is very mild and is often sold lightly smoked. In fancier restaurants, look for a dish called kasu cod: lightly smoked sablefish marinated in rice wine and quickly cooked.

SALMON

SALMON Salmon pump through Alaska like blood through a heart, bringing rhythmic, circulating nourishment to land, animals, and people. The predictable abundance of salmon allowed some Native cultures to flourish, and even today Alaskans continue to depend on salmon for subsistence and for the jobs created by annual returns of well over 150 million wild fish. Humans aren't the only beneficiaries of returning salmon: dead and dying spawners feed bears, eagles, other animals and birds, and, ultimately, the soil itself.

All five species of Pacific salmon spawn in Alaskan waters, and all are anadromous—that is, they spend part of their lives in freshwater and part at sea. After salmon hatch from their freshwater nests, or "redds," they undergo physiological changes that allow them to survive in salt water; these adapted juvenile salmon are called "smolts." When they're ready, smolts migrate to the ocean, where they grow up eating such fish as herring, capelin, and sand lance. Little is really known about the life of a salmon at sea, but we do know that after one to five years of ranging hundreds of miles, dodging hungry seals, orca whales, and fishing boats, mature salmon somehow find their way back to their natal streams to spawn and die. Smell seems to play a major role in the salmon's ability to find home.

While life cycles among the salmon are similar, the different species vary in how much time they spend in freshwater and at sea, and in what time of year they return to spawn. Because they return to so many different places, each salmon species is broken down into a multitude of "runs," grouped by home watershed—for instance, a "Copper River king" belongs to a different run than a "Kenai River king."

For the most part, Alaska's salmon are thriving, thanks to the absence of dams and overdevelopment, and to reasonable management. Whereas some runs of king and sockeye in the Lower 48 (most notably the Snake and Columbia Rivers) have been declared endangered, Alaska runs are still strong.

King or chinook salmon *(Oncorhynchus tshawytscha)* are the largest Pacific salmon, commonly weighing 30 pounds. The largest king on record, caught near Petersburg in 1949, weighed a whopping 126 pounds. Some Yukon River kings travel more than two thousand river miles in two months—never eating—to reach their spawning grounds high in the Yukon Territory. King salmon remain in Alaska's protected inside marine waters in the winter while the other four species move out to food-rich waters such as the Gulf of Alaska.

Chum or dog salmon *(O. keta),* averaging seven to eighteen pounds, are the most widespread of the Pacific salmon. People and lucky dogs both eat this fish; dried chum is a practical,

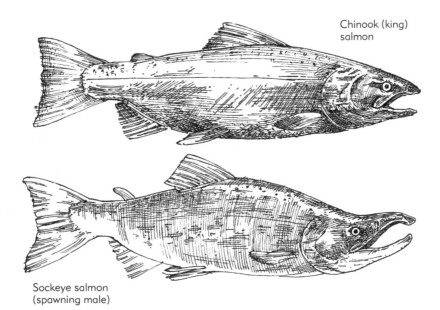

Chinook (king) salmon

Sockeye salmon (spawning male)

protein-rich food for sled dogs. This fact, plus the fact that spawning chum salmon grow an impressive set of teeth, probably account for the "dog" nickname.

Coho or silver salmon *(O. kisutch)* weigh between eight and twelve pounds, but can get much bigger. Healthy streams and tributaries are vitally important to coho, who might spend several years in freshwater rivers and streams before migrating out to sea. When large rivers flood, young coho use side waters to escape torrential currents; in severe cold weather, coho move into warmer, spring-fed streams to escape extremely low water temperatures.

> **Coho salmon might spend several years in freshwater before migrating to sea.**

Sockeye or red salmon *(O. nerka)* average four to eight pounds. Unlike the other salmon species, most sockeye runs occur in rivers with a lake at the head. The Kvichak River, which ends in Lake Iliamna, is home to one of the state's major sockeye runs. The kokanee is a landlocked, non-anadromous, smaller form of sockeye found only in lakes, generally from the Kenai Peninsula south.

Pinks, or humpies, or humpback salmon *(O. gorbuscha),* are the smallest, at about four pounds. They also spend the least amount of time in freshwater, traveling almost immediately to salt water after emerging from the gravel. Humpies also spend the least time at sea, returning in about two years.

SANDHILL CRANE
You will probably hear sandhill cranes before you see them: listen for the throaty, melodic, rattling *karrroook.* Whether they're passing overhead or feeding out of sight, the resonant sound of these birds in the distance will work on your brain until it registers: cranes.

The pewter-colored crane is a stately bird, standing about three feet tall. Cranes are often confused with great blue herons, but in Alaska, herons are limited to Southeast, are more closely associated with water, and are normally solitary birds. Sandhill cranes usually travel in groups and may be seen in tundra marshes, fields, tide flats, and muskeg of Western, Southwestern, and Interior Alaska. So the long-legged bird with the bright red forehead that you see dancing with others of its kind, *karrroook-*ing, is *Grus canadensis,* the sandhill crane. Cranes are famous for their dance—a leaping, twisting ballet that may be performed *à deux* or en masse. The nimble birds might dance anytime, anywhere, for any reason, although courtship seems to inspire particularly expressive moves.

Nests are a simple depression on the ground, lined with feathers and dried grass; both male and female incubate the eggs, usually two per pair. Nestlings can walk as soon as they hatch. Juveniles catch their own insects from an early age and adults are omnivorous—willing to eat just about anything they find, including frogs, insects, rodents, seeds, berries, roots, and aquatic invertebrates.

With their six-foot wingspans, cranes are magnificent fliers. Flocks circle into the air on rising thermals, assembling into Vs when they reach altitude, and traveling as far as 350 miles a day.

In all, about a quarter of a million sandhill cranes nest in Alaska—mostly on the Yukon–Kuskokwim Delta and northwest coast. Those two hundred thousand or more birds—who winter in Texas, New Mexico, and Mexico—funnel through the Tanana Valley, where up to fifty thousand migrants a day can be seen passing over the Delta Junction–Lake George area.

A smaller population of sandhill cranes nests near Bristol Bay and in the Susitna Valley. Most of those twenty thousand or so birds winter in California's Central Valley. Sandhill cranes like to roost at night standing in shallow water, and they also prefer wet areas for nesting. The loss of wetland habitat threatens the well-being of sandhill crane populations.

See also WETLAND

SEABIRDS Puffins, petrels, albatrosses, auklets, terns, shear-waters, fulmars, murrelets, murres, and gulls are all considered seabirds, a loose classification that includes birds that get their food from marine waters while swimming, skimming, or diving.

They spend most of their lives at sea, but since they can't very well lay eggs in the ocean, seabirds must come ashore to nest. Counting every foot of island, shore, and salt chuck, Alaska has about 47,300 miles of coastline, giving the long answer to the short question: What do one hundred million seabirds see in the Forty-ninth State? Fifty million seabirds nest here—more than in the rest of the entire Northern Hemisphere; the other fifty million just come for the food.

With all those birds demanding nesting sites, you might think things would get crowded, but fortunately, different species have different nesting preferences. Imagine, for instance, a small, rocky island off the coast: glaucous gulls nest on the flat ground on top; tufted puffins excavate burrows in the soil on the hillside while their cousins, the horned puffins, select nearby rock crevices. The common murre might like a cliff ledge, while kitti-wakes and cormorants are content on the cliff face itself. Farther below, auklets distribute themselves on the talus slopes and guillemots stick near the sea on boulder rubble.

Seabirds are the longest-lived among all the birds and hold the top five spots on the list of recorded maximum life spans of wild birds not in captivity. A Laysan albatross holds the record of thirty-seven years, five months, followed by an arctic tern of thirty-four, a great frigatebird of thirty, a western gull of nearly twenty-eight, and a 26½-year-old common murre.

SEALS Seals lounge in Alaska's waters and sun themselves on beaches and rocks like so many plump vacationers at the seashore. Unlike sea otters, who rarely leave the water, seals spend a fair amount of time "hauled out" on land or ice, resting and even giv-ing birth out of the water. At least seven seal species have been seen here: harbor, spotted, ringed, ribbon, bearded, hooded, and elephant seals. (The fur seal is really a sea lion.)

Ears and flippers set seals and sea lions apart. Seals have no external ear flaps, whereas sea lions have small, squirrel-like ears. On land, sea lions can turn their back flippers forward, allowing a lumbering sort of walking gait on land. Seals, however, don't have dexterous rear flippers, so must wriggle and hump in order to locomote while out of the water.

Bearded Seal The bearded seal *(Erignathus barbatus)* is the largest seal to commonly occur in Alaska's waters. At their heaviest in winter and early spring, the eight- to ten-foot seals may weigh more than 750 pounds. Found in the Bering, Chukchi, and Beaufort Seas, the tawny to dark brown seals remain important to coastal Natives even today. Bearded seals are reported to have the best-tasting meat, and their hide has been used to make boats, clothing, and rawhide bindings.

Adult bearded seals, which are almost always associated with sea ice, move seasonally with the ice pack, following receding ice north in the spring. Young seals may stay near ice-free bays and estuaries.

Yupik speakers call this seal *mukluk*. As the story goes, an early white explorer asked a Yupik person what he had on his feet and the man, thinking the explorer was asking what the material was, answered "mukluk," and to this day, Native-style boots are called mukluks. Inupiaq-speaking people call the bearded seal *oogruk*. The precise language also has names for a young *oogruk*—*oogruarokh*—and for an *oogruk* hauled out on the ice—*kamugituk*. In spring, when bearded seal males vocalize underwater songs, they are called *au-uk-touk*.

> Bearded seal hides have been used to make boats, clothing, and rawhide bindings.

It is said that when a young couple wanted to get together, they would go out to hunt the *oogruk*. If they were successful and got along, the match was approved.

Harbor Seal Of the seven species, you're most likely to see the harbor seal *(Phoca vitulina)*: a gray or brownish pudge, sometimes with spots or splotches, basking on icebergs, rocks, or beaches or curiously following a kayak. In Alaska, the four- to five-foot-long, 180-pound seals are found from Southeast up to Southwestern Alaska and throughout the Aleutian Islands. Harbor seals looking for a meal also occasionally follow fish into freshwater lakes, including Lake Iliamna in Southwestern Alaska, where the seals are seen year-round. Although they may readjust their locations somewhat from summer to winter, harbor seals are not considered migratory, and generally remain within 150 miles of where they were born.

Studies of harbor seals reveal a highly evolved physiological dive response that allows the air-breathing animals to stay underwater for more than twenty minutes. When the seal dives, its heart rate goes way down and blood is circulated only to the brain, lungs, and heart. In the rest of its body, high levels of myoglobin help bind oxygen in the muscles.

See also STELLER SEA LION

SHEEFISH   Sheefish look like they're plated in an armor of silvery gray ice—appropriate for a fish that lives only in the Far North. Having never before seen this cold-climate species, early French explorers called them *inconnu,* "unknown fish." Sheefish *(Stenodus leucicthys)* inhabit streams, rivers, and lakes in the northwestern part of Alaska. The largest member of the whitefish family, inconnu grow quite quickly for a high-latitude species. In fact, the biggest sheefish are found north of the Arctic Circle.

Inconnu tend to favor large, slow, murky rivers except during spawning season, when they migrate to fast, clear tributaries to lay their eggs. Some Yukon River sheefish travel up to one thousand miles to get to selected tributaries. As soon as spawning is complete, the fish move back down the rivers for the winter, sometimes as far as the river's delta, but not beyond.

> **Early French explorers called sheefish inconnu, "unknown fish."**

It appears that the long-lived sheefish spawn every other year. Most live at least ten years—some up to twenty and more—attaining weights of sixty pounds and lengths over three feet. They are generally abundant where they occur and have been an important traditional subsistence fish for some Alaska Native peoples. Inconnu fishing is catching on with sport anglers too, who call the fish "Eskimo tarpon" because of its large size and fighting ability.

SHOREBIRDS Amazing things come in small packages: shorebirds no bigger than sparrows undergo some of the most incredible migrations in the bird world. Many travel from the Arctic to South America and back again in a year—sometimes at altitudes of ten thousand feet, often flying nonstop, a thousand miles at a time. About forty-eight species of shorebird visit Alaska; most come in the spring to nest, then migrate out of state for the winter.

Generally speaking, shorebirds are the smallish birds that run and wade along the water's edge feeding on aquatic invertebrates—not to be confused with large, "stalking" wading birds like herons. Shorebirds can be found on any shore, including seashores and the shores of inland lakes and rivers. The largest species, such as the black oystercatcher *(Haematopus bachmani)* and whimbrel *(Numenius phaeopus),* are about the size of a gull. The least sandpiper *(Calidris minutilla),* the smallest shorebird, is about the size of a chickadee.

Shorebirds have the habit of congregating in huge numbers at specific sites along the migration route. These "staging areas" are usually mudflats or similar habitats with a superabundance of worms and other invertebrate foods. A handful of critical staging areas located around the United States support millions of North American shorebirds in their annual migrations. Without these special areas, bird populations would collapse. Alaska's Copper River Delta is such a place, hosting about 20 million shorebirds a year. Virtually the entire population of western sandpipers *(C. mauri)* stops at the Copper River Delta to rest and feed before spreading out to nest in the Yukon–Kuskokwim Delta and elsewhere along the state's west coast.

Because each species of shorebird is built a little differently, the birds aren't in fierce competition for food, even where they occur in great concentrations. For example, in tidal areas, birds sort themselves out as the tide recedes. The least sandpipers stay high in the tide zone, poking about in the drier mud; the slightly larger, longer-billed dunlins *(C. alpina)* follow the receding tide a bit farther to wetter mud. The even larger, longer-billed, longer-legged dowitchers *(Limnodromus* spp.) go wading, using their long bills to probe through the water for food.

SHRIMP Although king crab may be the archetypal Alaska crustacean, the state has more than its share of shrimp too: the world's greatest concentrations of pink shrimp are found in the Gulf of Alaska.

In all, sixty species of shrimp live in Alaska's waters; members of the *Pandalus* genus are familiar as some of America's most-consumed seafood. Pink shrimp *(Pandalus borealis)*, the smallest pandalids, show up over ice in shrimp cocktails. Another species, spot shrimp *(P. platyceros)*, is invited to all the best barbecues. Spots are the largest shrimp in the North Pacific—up to eleven inches long, sword-nose to tail.

In the ocean, spots are usually found around rock piles and coral at about 360 feet. Pinks prefer muddy bottoms anywhere from 60 feet to 4,800 feet deep. Spots, pinks, and the other pandalids (humpies, sidestripes, and coonstripes) migrate seasonally between deep and shallow water, and often move up and down in the water column on a daily basis, spending the day on the bottom and moving up through the water at night to feed on diatoms, algae, and various other invertebrates. Shrimp also scavenge dead organic matter.

Pandalid shrimp distinguish themselves in other ways than in a Louie—they are among the few animals in the world that are commonly hermaphroditic. Most juveniles develop as males. But

Pink shrimp

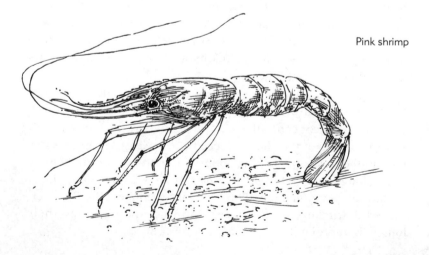

after a season or two as a spawning male, the shrimp goes through a short transition and becomes fully female, and stays that way for the rest of its five- to six-year life span.

Just prior to the reproductive season, females molt into shells customized for carrying eggs. In spawning, male and female grasp each other while the male deposits a packet of sperm on the female's underside. The female then carries her cluster of up to four thousand fertilized eggs until they hatch.

SITKA BLACK-TAILED DEER
There is an old saying: A pine needle fell. The eagle saw it, the bear smelled it, the deer heard it.

Sitka black-tailed deer are the ears of Alaska's coastal forests. The only deer native to the Northland, Sitka black-tailed deer *(Odocoileus hemionus sitkensis)* were originally found only in Southeast, but have been successfully transplanted to other places in Alaska including Prince William Sound and Kodiak Island.

Smaller than their closest Lower 48 cousins, mule deer *(O. hemionus)* and Columbian black-tailed deer *(O. hemionus columbianus)*, Sitka does and bucks average 80 and 120 pounds respectively, and are typically less than three feet tall at the shoulder. They get their name from the spot of black dabbing the tips of their tails. As with all deer family members except caribou, only the males have antlers. Compared to other antlered animals both in and outside Alaska, the antlers of Sitka black-tailed bucks are relatively small.

Coming from Southeast, the land of water, it's natural that Sitka deer should be good swimmers. Their willingness to get wet allowed them to spread throughout the region's countless islands. In general, wolves are the major predators, although grizzly and black bears also prey on deer. Human hunters take their share too, but the most serious threat to Alaska's deer comes from loss of winter habitat.

Sitka black-tails depend on mature forests for their survival. The multilayered canopy of old growth allows enough light for understory forage plants such as blueberry and bunchberry to grow. And in winter, the canopy prevents snow from getting too deep on the forest floor, so deer can find food under the shelter of the trees. Unfortunately, a replanted grown-up clear-cut isn't the same as old growth. Same-age trees usually grow together so densely that understory food plants can't get enough light to sustain themselves, let alone hungry deer.

Deer occupy a cultural, as well as ecological, niche in Alaska. Following a war between two clans, coastal Native peoples sometimes held a peace, or "deer," ceremony in which symbolic hostages were taken. These "guest hostages" were called "deer" in honor of the animal's gentle, guileless nature.

See also HORNS AND ANTLERS

SNAKES AND OTHER REPTILES It's as if Saint
Patrick himself had come through Alaska, driving out the snakes like he did in Ireland. Basically, Alaska is snake-free, although Saint Paddy may have missed one or two; garter snakes (*Thamnophis* spp.) have been reported along the Taku and Stikine Rivers in Southeast.

Because the cold-blooded snakes and lizards rely so totally on sunshine to warm themselves, digest their food, and hatch their eggs, the long, dark Alaskan winters quash the possibility of viable reptile populations.

Of course, every rule has an exception. Two reptiles that are occasionally seen swimming through Alaskan marine waters are the leatherback *(Dermochelys coriacea)* and green *(Chelonia mydas)* sea turtles. These turtles are thought to travel to Alaska with the warm Japan and North Pacific currents, which arrive at Southeast from the open ocean, then flow northwest through the Gulf of Alaska to the Aleutian Islands.

Obviously, other cold-blooded creatures—wood frogs, fish, and many insects, for instance—have adapted to northern life, but for snakes and lizards, Alaska is the end of the earth.

SNOW FLEA Seeing a million minuscule insects swarming
over a field of snow might make you itch, but snow fleas aren't interested in you or any other warm-blooded mammal. That's

because these wingless, six-legged smidgens aren't fleas at all: they're springtails (order Collembola). The name comes from the springing organ, or "furcula," folded up under the springtail's abdomen and held by a sort of catch. When the catch is released, the furcula snaps back, catapulting the 1/16-inch insect into the air.

Springtails, of which there are many species, are among the most numerous of insects whose range extends into the Arctic. It's no wonder—physiological adaptations allow springtails to survive being frozen solid within a glacier for up to three years.

> Snow fleas can survive being frozen solid within a glacier for up to three years.

Some busy scientist figured out that in richer soils of the Far North, springtails and mites, the other major arctic bug, can form a biomass of about thirty-four thousand pounds per square mile. And who are among the hungry predators exploiting this lively, mitey mass? Spiders and centipedes.

As for themselves, snow fleas eat mold, decaying vegetation, algae, and sometimes each other—but never you or your husky.

SNOWSHOE HARE

Snowshoe hares scream when they're in trouble, thump-drum their huge hind feet, and perform aerial somersaults in the throes of courtship—but otherwise, life is basically one unending reproductive cycle.

This fruitfulness is appreciated by foxes, wolves, owls, and especially lynx, all of whom rely on the nonhibernating hares as a reliable source of winter food. Female hares begin breeding when they're about a year old, and have two to three litters of four to six young annually. Snowshoe hares don't dig nests or burrows, preferring the simpler shelter of a bush or brush pile. Young hares, called "leverets," are born in a shallow, unlined scrape in the ground called a "form." The two-ounce babies are born fully furred with their eyes open and are able to walk by the time their fur has dried (unlike rabbits, who are born helpless, hairless, and blind). They are weaned from their mother and eating vegetation in less than two weeks.

Snowshoe hares *(Lepus americanus)* are found in spruce forests, wet woodlands, and brushy areas throughout Alaska except the North Slope and some western parts of the state. Larger than cottontails, the "varying" hares, as they're also called, are about twenty inches long and weigh three to four pounds. The larger tundra or arctic hares *(L. timidus)* are found on windy, rocky slopes and dry upland tundra from the North Slope all the way around the state's western perimeter onto the Alaska Peninsula. The "Alaskan hare," as it's also called, can be more than two feet long and weigh up to twelve pounds.

Both species are yellowish brown in the summer, turn white in winter, and have ultra-furry, snowshoe-like hind feet. When a hare hops, its hind feet plunk down in front of its front feet; hare tracks can be confusing because the rear, big-paw prints are forward, indicating the direction of the hare's movement.

The hares' boom-and-bust populations seem to cycle every ten years or so. At their peak, as many as six hundred hares may occupy a single square mile. Population crashes are most likely due to a combination of dwindling food, disease and stress brought on by overcrowding, and pressure from predator populations flourishing because of the burgeoning hare populations.

Hares and rabbits are not rodents; they are in a separate order, Lagomorpha.

See also LYNX

SNOWY OWL Snowy owls look like scrimshawed ivory figures, their white bodies etched with a black or brown feather-tip pattern.

One of the largest owls in North America, the two-foot snowy *(Nyctea scandiaca)* hunts by day. When the ground is covered with snow, the owl relies heavily on its keen sense of hearing. A disk of stiff facial feathers and fleshy ear flaps work together to funnel sound into the owl's ears. Right and left ear openings are shaped differently to help the owl determine where a sound is coming from: over there, the sound of a vole running in its tunnel under the snow. The ivory figure swoops silently to pluck the sound— the vole, the meal—from the snow with strong talons.

Its presence in an area depends largely on the presence of

Snowy owl
(juvenile)

lemmings, the snowy owl's major prey. If lemmings are abundant enough in a given year, snowy owls will overwinter as far north as the Arctic. The lives of the two animals are so intertwined that the male owl holds a dead lemming while he performs his stiff courtship dance. In years when lemmings are extremely scarce, snowy owls may forgo reproduction.

Snowy owls nest on treeless coastal tundra from the western Aleutians to the arctic tundra of Northern Alaska. They nest on the ground, ready to defend their territory against wolves, foxes, and humans. Because snowy owls so fiercely protect their nesting territory, geese and eider ducks often select nesting sites of their own near owls'.

See also LEMMING AND VOLE

STEELHEAD For many sport anglers, steelhead are the pot of gold at the end of the fishing rainbow. In actuality, they *are* the rainbow—steelhead *(Salmo gairdneri)* are an oceangoing form of rainbow trout (also *S. gairdneri)*. Although they look quite similar, steelhead are generally heavier, but appear more streamlined than rainbows. Alaska boasts hundreds of productive coastal steelhead streams, from Dixon Entrance around the Gulf of Alaska north to Cold Bay.

"Resident rainbows" stay in freshwater all their lives, but, perhaps at the whispered urging of genes—no one knows for sure—steelhead take the anadromous path, migrating out to salt water at about age two. They remain at sea for up to four years before returning to home waters to spawn. For every hundred juveniles that go out, only five or ten foil the marine gauntlet of hungry whales, seals, sea lions, and human fishers to return to their natal stream. Of the ones that do make it back, about a quarter (mostly female) survive the rigors of reproduction. After eggs are laid and fertilized, the tired survivors head back to salt water to renew themselves. They will return the next season—and possibly two or three more seasons—to spawn.

Out in the ocean, eating squids and fishes, steelhead grow faster and larger than their stay-at-home rainbow counterparts. Although any steelhead over fifteen pounds and thirty-two inches long is considered a prize fish, steelhead can grow much larger: the state's record steelhead was more than forty-two pounds.

STELLER SEA LION Not only does Alaska have North America's biggest moose and biggest bears, but the largest sea lions live here too. On average, Steller sea lion bulls are nearly eleven feet long and can weigh eighteen hundred pounds. Females weigh about half as much as the gargantuan bulls, even though they're only two to three feet shorter. The efficient predators grow so huge on a diet of pollock, cod, herring, salmon, squid, and octopus.

In the spring, bulls "haul out" on rocky offshore islands to claim breeding turf. Bulls don't eat during the breeding period, turning their full attention to the cows and to aggressive defense of their territory from other bulls. Most fights are restrained affairs for display purposes only, but serious clashes do occasionally occur. Cows basically ignore the goings on between bulls and move about as they please, even though a bull may try to herd a female back into his own territory. Females generally give birth to one pup during this time and mate again shortly afterward—sometimes giving birth in the territory of one male and mating in another. After mating, the fertilized egg doesn't implant and begin growing until about October. This allows breeding to occur when males are around, but ensures that birthing is synchronized with other females and timed for the following spring.

Steller sea lions (*Eumetopias jubatus*) occur throughout the North Pacific from Alaska to Japan. In Alaska—home to 70 percent to 80 percent of the world's depleting population—Steller sea lions are found in coastal areas of Southeast, the Gulf of Alaska, Aleutian Islands, and Bering Sea.

In the 1970s, scientists estimated the Steller population worldwide at around 281,000 but that number has dropped at about 80 percent over the last three decades. The reason for the decline is unclear. Many possible causes have been tested and eliminated, including pollution, climate changes, and entanglement in marine debris. Scientists are now investigating the possibility that sea lions are losing the competition for food to commercial trawler fisheries that target the pollock, herring, and other schooling fish on which sea lions subsist.

Historically, Steller sea lions were an important resource to Native peoples, particularly those living on the Aleutian Islands, who hunted the lions for food, clothing, boots, and boat coverings. Steller sea lion whiskers were also once used by the Chinese to clean opium pipes.

Protected under the Marine Mammal Protection Act, Steller sea lions were listed as a threatened species in 1990. A western subpopulation was listed as endangered in 1999.

Georg Steller, a German naturalist-explorer, was with Vitus Bering when that Danish sea captain explored the region in the

Steller sea lion

early eighteenth century. Steller was the first European to describe the giant sea lion named for its lion-like roar and thick, mane-like ruff.

SWAN In 1932, there were only sixty-nine trumpeter swans left in the Lower 48. Market hunters of the late nineteenth and early twentieth centuries had nearly wiped out the statuesque bird to meet market demands for its meat and the feathered skins that were used to make powder puffs. Those sixty-nine birds, which were protected by the establishment of a refuge near Yellowstone National Park, seemed to represent the entire remaining world population of *Cygnus buccinator.* But in 1958, biologists identified over fifteen hundred trumpeter swans nesting in the remote territory of Alaska. Eggs from Alaska's trumpeter swans have been used for restoration programs in the Lower 48, and now the world population numbers over eighteen thousand—80 percent of which still breed in Alaska. The trumpeter swan is the largest waterfowl on earth: males average twenty-eight pounds, but can weigh up to forty pounds; females are slightly smaller. Wingspans spread six to eight feet.

Trumpeters nest in Interior and Southcentral Alaska, preferring marshy sites adjacent to small lakes. Nests are platform mounds—often built right in the marsh to be surrounded by water—and may be six to twelve feet in diameter. Pairs mate for life and like to use the same nest year after year. Females, called "pens," lay an average of four eggs and incubate the clutch while the male "cob" defends the nest. Both parents care for the "cygnets" until they are about fifteen weeks old and ready to fly. In the fall, the family migrates south together to spend the winter along the Pacific Northwest coast, appearing to hold up the sky with their great wings and angelic presence.

> The trumpeter swan is the largest waterfowl on earth.

Alaska's other swan, the tundra or whistling swan *(C. columbianus),* was never in quite the peril the trumpeter swan was, but it also suffered at the hands of market hunters. Today, about 160,000 tundra swans nest in the Northern and Western regions of Alaska and the Canadian Arctic. Hundreds winter on the Alaska Peninsula, but the rest of the population splits itself between eastern wintering grounds in North Carolina and a western winter range that stretches from southern British Columbia to central California.

Tundra swans are about two-thirds smaller than trumpeters, but it's difficult to tell them apart just by looking at them. Voice is the best clue: trumpeter swans sound a loud call, as clear and sonorous as a French horn—more musical than the higher-pitched warbly sound gabbled by tundra swans.

TERN Can you imagine putting twelve thousand miles on your car in a single trip, then turning around three months later and doing it again? Arctic terns travel up to twenty-four thousand miles a year—migrating from the Antarctic to the Arctic in spring, and back again in the fall. This tern version of endless summer gives the champion travelers more sunlight hours during the year than perhaps any other animal on earth.

About the size of a slender robin, terns are built for speed and agility with long, narrow, pointed wings, a forked tail, and a sleek, streamlined body. Although terns have webbed toes, their feet are small, making them relatively poor swimmers. So, taking advantage of their nimble flying skills, terns hover easily over the water looking for fish to catch. Spotting a target, terns plunge in, snatch the goods, and retake the air so quickly they barely get their feathers wet.

Of Alaska's three tern species, arctic terns are by far the most numerous and widespread. With their bright red bills and feet, black caps, white cheeks, and soft-gray backs, arctic terns are among the snappiest-looking of all seabirds. *Sterna paradisaea* nest in relatively small colonies on tide flats, beaches, meadows, or tundra from Southeast through the Interior to the Arctic Coast. Although the nests aren't elaborate—merely a slight depression scraped in the ground for their two eggs—arctic terns defend their nests aggressively and seem willing to attack any intruder, animal or human.

Biologists believe that the pair bonds formed between individual males and females during breeding season loosen during the winter, but that the same pairs reestablish themselves every nesting season. In courtship, the male flies over the female showing her fish he's caught. If she's receptive, he begins to feed her. This feeding seems to have the threefold effect of strengthening the pair bond, inducing copulation, and supplying the female with extra nutrition to meet the energy demands of laying eggs.

Both parents incubate the eggs and feed the young when they hatch. Less than three months later, the family begins its southward migration. Apparently, there is no dawdling—one arctic tern tagged up north was recaptured less than three months later, eleven thousand miles away.

WALRUS Talk about overbite. The walrus's ivory appendages are basically outsized canine teeth. Both males and females have the tusks—useful tools whose primary function is to help the eight- to ten-foot, one- to two-ton animals pull themselves up onto land or ice floes. The walrus's scientific name, *Odobenus rosmarus,* means "tooth walker." A bull walrus generally has larger tusks than a cow; tusks can grow over a yard long.

Tusks also serve as status symbols, defensive weapons, and ice hammers. Walruses don't dig for food with the tusks; instead, to find clams, crabs, and other bottom-dwelling invertebrates, a walrus uses its sensitive muzzle and whiskers to feel along the seafloor to detect edibles small as a grape. The walrus uses its piston-like tongue to suck meat from shells—an efficient way to consume the one hundred to two hundred pounds of food the huge animal eats every day.

Walruses often collect in family groups of one bull, two or three cows, and a few calves; bulls sing complex underwater songs to attract the attention of cows. Because gestation is long, about fifteen months, females breed every other year or so. Calves, which can weigh 100 to 160 pounds at birth, stay with their mothers eighteen months to 2½ years. Cows are fiercely protective and have been known to carry injured calves away from danger on their backs. Predators include humans, polar bears, and orca whales.

In Alaska, walruses range from the Alaska Peninsula to Point Barrow, usually in relatively shallow water near land or ice. They remain in Alaskan waters all year, drifting north with receding sea ice in the spring and back as ice extends southward in the fall.

Northern peoples traditionally made their boats from walrus hide. They also ate the meat, used the intestines to make rain gear, and carved the tusks into harpoon heads, knife handles, dolls, and other tools and artwork. Alaska Natives still hunt walrus, especially people from villages near the Bering Strait. Only Natives may hunt walrus, and only verified Native-made ivory articles can be sold to non-Natives.

> **Walrus tusks serve as status symbols, defensive weapons, and ice hammers.**

WHALES A long, long time ago, whale ancestors walked the earth. For some unknown reason, some unknown millions of years ago, they waded back into the sea and stayed there. Their nostrils eventually migrated to the top of their head, front limbs turned into flippers, ears and back legs disappeared, and a flat, horizontal tail developed. But even after all this time, they've kept the lungs, though it means holding their breath under water.

Now that the whaling days are largely over, Alaska is a more hospitable place for these intriguing marine mammals. More than fourteen whale species have been observed in Great Land waters, including humpback and gray whales, narwhals, orcas, belugas, bowheads, and blues. Two of the whale species most likely to be seen—because of their numbers, habits, and preferred habitats—are the orcas, or killer whales, and humpbacks.

Whales are divided into two major groups: toothed whales and baleen whales. Beluga and sperm whales are examples of toothed whales, and orcas are also commonly placed in this group, even though they're actually huge dolphins.

Humpback whales belong to the baleen group. Baleen grows in long strips from the whale's upper gumline and is made of keratin, the same substance found in horns, hooves, fish scales, and fingernails. Baleen whales take enormous amounts of water into their mouth, then push the water out through the baleen screen to trap floating food such as small fish and tiny shrimp-like organisms known as krill. Native peoples use baleen to weave strong baskets and create artwork.

Humpback Whale Unlike most of the other baleen whales, humpbacks *(Megaptera novaeangliae)* are very vocal. Only males sing. Suspended in the water with heads bowed and pec-toral ("arm") fins outstretched, they perform songs of two to eight identifiable phrases, always in the same order. Some bulls sing up to seven hours straight, pausing only to surface for a breath of air, almost always at the same point in the song sequence. The hump-backs' voices have an entrancing range of pitch, tone, texture, and nuance. Vocalizations are thought to be a way for bulls to express their social status. Loose but possibly long-lasting group associa-tions have been observed among humpback whales.

Besides being accomplished vocalists, humpbacks (who enjoy herring and other small schooling fish along with krill) are clever hunters, catching fish with a technique known as bubble-netting. To bubble-net, one or more whales blow bubbles while

Humpback whale

swimming in circles below a school of fish. When the fish ball up in the middle of the bubbles, the whales swim up through the mass with their mouths open.

The multitalented humpback is also a great performance artist. More gymnastic than the other baleen whales, they engage in a variety of aquatic acrobatics, including hurling their forty-seven-foot, thirty-ton bodies almost completely out of the water in a spectacular leaping display known as breaching.

Humpbacks may be seen in any season in Alaska, but most migrate to Mexico or Hawaii and other Pacific Islands for the winter, traveling in pods of two to five individuals. In the summer, they are concentrated in Southeast, Prince William Sound, an area north of Kodiak Island, and areas of the Aleutian Islands and southern Bering Sea.

Orca Whale Orca *(Orcinus orca)* society is extremely complex. Most individuals belong to family pods with definite home ranges ("resident" pods), but there are also wider-traveling "transient" pods about which little is known. Both resident and transient orcas occur in Alaska's waters and are most common in waters over the continental shelf from Southeast through the Aleutian Islands, and north into the Chukchi and Beaufort Seas, from where they retreat in the fall when sea ice advances.

Resident pods are matriarchal; sons and daughters stay with their mother for her forty- to eighty-year life span. When a pod grows too large, or an old female dies, the pod splits or continues along matrilineal lines. Mating in the wild has never been observed, but families periodically come together in superpods, during which time mating may occur; long-lasting male-female pairs are apparently not formed.

Each resident pod uses a distinct dialect and possesses an extensive range of vocalizations. The North Pacific transients, which range from Alaska at least as far south as central California, all speak the same dialect. Transient orcas appear to be more aggressive than residents, preying on sea lions, seals, sharks, porpoises, adult and juvenile whales of other species, and, in at least one case, a swimming moose. Resident orcas eat mostly fish.

WOLF Wolves are wildness personified, loping silently, fluidly, through the woods, over the snow, mile after mile.

Wolves have been part of Alaska's ecosystem for nearly half a million years: hunting, being hunted, revered and reviled—living in territory staked out near our own at the top of the food chain. The widespread presence of wolves confirms the sense that Alaska is still an undomesticated place.

Gray wolves *(Canus lupus)* range throughout Alaska's mainland from the North Slope to Southcentral, and into the Aleutians and Southeast. They roam in a wide variety of habitats, including arctic tundra, coastal rain forests, and shrubby areas of the Interior. In Southeast, wolves are generally dark colored; throughout the rest of Alaska, gray or black is the most common color, although gray wolves can also be white, tan, or anywhere on the black-tan-white scale.

> The presence of wolves confirms the sense that Alaska is still undomesticated.

Highly social, wolves live in tight-knit, well-organized packs of half a dozen or so animals, usually comprising an "alpha" or dominant breeding pair and their offspring. Larger packs of up to thirty animals include extended-family relatives and possibly a few unrelated individuals. Males and females have separate hierarchical social ranks. Alpha males enforce order among male pack members; alpha females keep other females in line. The alpha female is most aggressive about her exclusive right to breed. It appears that the alpha male and female share pack leadership, particularly in travel and hunting decisions.

As social animals, wolves need to be able to communicate with each other, and this they do very well, employing both verbal and nonverbal cues. Whimpering or whining is a friendly sound; growling intends to be threatening; barking signals an alarm. And howling is . . . howling. Among other things, howling bonds the pack, expresses satisfaction with life, claims territory, and cries, "Here I am, where are you?"

Pack communication is largely conveyed through facial expression, body language, and tail signals. How high a wolf holds its tail corresponds with how confident it feels.

Eye contact is another indication of rank: dominant animals use unyielding stares to intimidate lesser pack members. An angry wolf bares its teeth and pricks up its ears; a suspicious wolf pulls its ears back and squints. When a wolf is afraid, its ears flatten against its head.

Wolf pups are born deaf and blind, but have developed enough to venture out of the den by the time they're three weeks old. Every wolf in the pack participates in rearing the alpha pair's litter. Each day, pack members range out to find food while the mother stays with her offspring. The hunters eat their fill, then return to the den and regurgitate tenderized meat for the pups and nursing female. As the pups get older, adults begin bringing intact prey to share. By fall, youngsters are ready to travel with the group. They join in the hunt at about a year old.

Moose and caribou are the main prey of mainland wolves, although Dall sheep are also sometimes taken. In Southeast, wolves prey mostly on Sitka black-tailed deer, beaver, and mountain goats. When large prey animals are unavailable, wolves turn to small mammals like voles, ground squirrels, snowshoe hares, lemmings, and occasionally birds and fish.

Under well-balanced ecological conditions, predation by wolves keeps big-game animal populations at a size appropriate for the available habitat; this doesn't necessarily mean that fewer big-game animals will be available for human hunters. But if weather or some other factor causes big-game populations to plummet, competition between humans and wolves may escalate. Alaskan guides and hunters—many of whom care about the well-being of wolves—work to find ways to meet their own economic needs and fulfill their hunting traditions while ensuring that wolves will be howling on the Last Frontier into perpetuity.

WOLVERINE Wolverines are born to be riled. Extremely powerful for its size, *Gulo gulo* (loosely translated from the Latin to mean "glutton") is a get-out-of-my-way kind of animal that will do just about anything for a meal, including break into cabins, steal bait and snared animals from traps, eat frozen carrion, and occasionally kill a moose or caribou.

This largest terrestrial member of the Mustelidae family (which includes weasels and sea otters) looks like a bushy-tailed cross between a badger and a bear, with thick brown fur marked by two creamy stripes along each side. Males weigh twenty to forty-five pounds; females average fifteen to thirty pounds.

Primarily a scavenger, the wolverine has powerful jaws for eating the frozen meat of winter-killed animals, and large teeth to crush the bones and skin of carcasses left behind by wolves and bears. But if the carrion pickings are slim, wolverines are fully capable of hunting their own squirrels, snowshoe hares, ptarmigan, marmots, and, under rare circumstances, moose, mountain goats, and caribou.

Wolverines are very solitary animals, coming together only for a brief mating season. Males stake out territories of up to 240 square miles and travel up to 40 miles a day in search of food; females maintain smaller territories of 50 to 100 square miles. Because the species requires expansive tracts of undisturbed, forested wilderness, wolverines have all but disappeared from most of their historical range in the Lower 48. But in Alaska, the "carcajou" is still distributed across most of mainland Alaska and some parts of Southeast.

Northern peoples have long favored wolverine fur to trim their parka hoods. Not only is it thick and beautiful, but the

Wolverine

tapered guard hairs shed frost better than any other fur. Wolverine fur is quite durable as well; the hairs don't break or pull out, even after years of service. On the overall fur quality scale of 100, wolverine is rated 100 (a top honor it shares with its cousin the sea otter).

See also MUSTELIDS

WOOD FROG It's a big leap, but small frogs do live in the Far North. The wood frog *(Rana sylvatica)* is the only North American amphibian living in the Arctic. Widely distributed on both sides of the Arctic Circle, the three-inch frog is found from north of the Brooks Range to Southeast, in muskeg, tundra, and forests. Wood frogs manage winter by sleeping through it, under a blanket of dead vegetation and snow. Winter mortality is high, but even so, wood frogs are abundant. Which is good, because *something* needs to help eat all those mosquitoes. In turn, the frogs are eaten by birds and other small animals. When under attack by shrews, the wood frog emits what has been scientifically described as a "mercy scream." Research doesn't indicate whether the scream works or not. The wood frog male's spring mating song is an abrupt, almost quacking call.

Wood frogs have smooth, light brown to gray, spotted or otherwise patterned skin and a cream-colored belly. Most have a dark eye mask and a stripe running down the back. Four other amphibians live in Alaska (out of thirty-three hundred species worldwide): the spotted frog *(R. pretiosa)*, the western or boreal toad *(Bufo boreas)*, the long-toed salamander *(Ambystoma macrodactylum)*, and the rough-skinned newt *(Taricha granulosa)*.

WOOLLY MAMMOTH AND BLUE BABE

Lions and tigers eating hairy elephants and camels? In Alaska? It seems odd to us now, but tens of thousands of years ago, when huge expanses of North America were covered by glaciers, large parts of Interior Alaska were ice-free. A wide variety of grazing and predatory animals took refuge on this open, grassy plain. It's possible that increasingly efficient human hunters contributed to the demise of Alaska's large mammals eight thousand to ten thousand years ago, but most likely a combination of factors—especially a changing environment—led to their extinction.

Some of those ancient animals have been preserved in layers of perpetually frozen ground that might lie under a hundred feet of soil. These "ice lenses" offer incredible views of the past. Remains of prehistoric woolly mammoths, mastodons, saber-toothed tigers, lions, bison, horses, and camels have all been recovered from such sites in the Forty-ninth State.

Remains of prehistoric woolly mammoths have been recovered from frozen ground in Alaska.

One of the most amazing discoveries was Blue Babe, a male steppe bison *(Bison priscus)* that now lies in state at the University of Alaska Fairbanks Museum. Blue Babe still wears most of his wrinkled hide—and his ears and nose, hooves and horns—all of which have taken on a bluish hue due to mineralization. The unfortunate Babe died about thirty-six thousand years ago, probably killed by a lion, judging from claw and tooth puncture marks. He was uncovered near Fairbanks in 1979 by gold miners.

Keeping Blue Babe company at the museum are remains and replicas of woolly mammoths and mastodons. Both are essentially hairy elephants, but the mammoth was the larger of the two, standing up to fourteen feet tall at the shoulder, with upward-curling tusks that grew to thirteen feet. Mammoth remains are much more common in the Tanana Valley than are the remains of mastodons.

Woolly mammoths were grazing machines. These gigantic herbivores could grow new teeth when the old ones ground down—scientists believe some individuals wore out as many as six sets of teeth.

See also BERINGIA; BISON; HUMAN SETTLEMENT

TWO

Plants

ACROSS ALASKA, when the snow and gray of winter roll back, the land is green: forest green, herbal green, gray-green, every green. The whites and grays of summer reside in birch and aspen trunks, and wildflowers wash the land with bursts of yellow, magenta, purple, blue, and pink. In the fall, a brief blaze of gold and red burns fleetingly across the leaves of the bushes and trees.

From the two-hundred-foot-tall Sitka spruce to the two-inch arctic forget-me-not, Alaska has more than fifteen hundred species of trees, shrubs, wildflowers, mosses, ferns, grasses, and other growing green things—a good number for a northern climate, although not as diverse as a tropical jungle, where one square mile may contain three thousand different species.

It's as hard to generalize about Alaska's plants as it is to generalize about the animals or the land itself. Dense old-growth forests flourish in the moderate marine climate of Southeast, but just as oxygen gets thinner at high altitudes, trees thin out dramatically at progressively higher latitudes. Alaska has fewer tree species than any other state. Of the thirty-three native trees, only twelve grow more than seventy feet tall; nine of those twelve species grow only in Southeast.

Moving higher in latitude is like moving higher in elevation on a mountain; traveling from Southeast into the Interior and past the Arctic Circle, you will notice the forests thinning out and trees getting smaller and then stunted-looking as shrubs, low-growing plants, grasses, and lichens become more prevalent on the landscape. On the Far North Arctic plain, trees disappear altogether.

A number of Alaskan plants, including the arctic forget-me-not (a subspecies of the state flower), won't be seen anywhere else in the United States, but most of Alaska's tree and plant species also occur in areas of the Lower 48—although the Alaskan representatives do seem to have their own look: the devil's club appears bigger, the willows thicker, the fireweed showier. After all, a plant growing in Alaska has significantly different growing parameters than the same plant growing in

California, so it's reasonable to believe the Northland plant will have a different quality (an exuberance, perhaps?), even if you can't quite put your finger on what it is.

Alaskan plants have adapted to growing in spurts during the short but light-intensive summers. Studies have shown that a white spruce in Alaska and a white spruce in Massachusetts both grow about the same amount in a given cycle, but the Alaska tree's growth occurs in about half the time.

Even on cool summer days, a plant is feeding itself the whole time the sun is above the horizon. Photosynthesis, the process by which a plant uses solar power to transform carbon dioxide into sugars to feed itself, depends on sunlight, not sun temperatures. A University of Alaska professor has said that northcentral Alaska has "the highest [summer] potential for photosynthesis of any region in the world."

Still, a short growing season makes it impractical for many species to rely solely on reproduction through seed, so a number of northern plants spread through roots or runners. The small, flowering bunchberry plant, for instance, produces seeds but assures its propagation in less than ideal circumstances by sending out rhizomes as well. Roots are important to Alaskan plants for other reasons too. Surface debris takes much longer to compost in the north, so soils are frequently nutrient-poor. Northern plants often have more extensively developed root systems than their southern relations, because complex roots are more efficient at obtaining minerals.

Nutrition isn't the only challenge. On the tundra or above tree line in the mountains, where drying winds are likely to be a threat, plants grow low to the ground in cushions or mats, often covering themselves with "hair" or tough skin to prevent water loss. Moss campion lies like a fluffy pancake on the ground, hunkering below the wind. Air temperature within the plant's cushion can be 40°F warmer than air temperature at shin level.

The tamarack tree has an innovative way to deal with winter: this deciduous conifer sheds its needles so they won't transpire away moisture in desiccating winds and cold. Bare branches also accumulate less snow, so the tree is better able to avoid storm damage. In areas of permafrost, or permanently frozen ground, the taproots of trees such as spruce spread out instead of growing straight down.

Even within their own groups, Alaskan plants customize to fit into their specific climatic region and habitat—be it the rain forest of Southeast, Interior river valley, or Arctic muskeg. For instance, Alaska has about fifty-six separate willow species, from the inches-high netleaf willow of the Arctic tundra to the thirty-foot-tall littletree willow of Southcentral streamsides.

Alaska may not have a jungle-sized selection of plants, but each priceless species has a purpose on the land. Many have a purpose in the lives of Alaska's animals and people too—as food, medicine, and useful material.

Green plants are food factories. They feed themselves and in turn offer their manufactured carbohydrates to all of us non-photosynthesizing creatures who must eat our food. Alaskans eat the flowers of fireweed, the fruits of roses, and the bulbs of chocolate lilies. Moose eat willows; bears eat grass; grouse eat spruce needles. Even animals that are completely carnivorous, like weasels, benefit from green plants every time they eat an herbivorous vole. And if nobody eats the plants, their nutrients are eventually returned to the soil for recycling.

Many Alaska Native peoples believed that, in the beginning, all things possessed spirits—even the plants. Herbal medicines were vitally important to the physical and emotional well-being of the people. Tlingit tradition has it that shamans were first alerted to the medicinal power of devil's club when they observed bears wallowing in the roots to soothe their wounds.

Although they are quieter than howling wolves and screeching seabirds, Alaska's plants are not without voice. They speak in the whisper of aspen leaves and the pop of lupine seedpods, if you know how to listen.

ALDER Just as Alaska's human history is full of pioneers, so is its natural history. One of the most important colonists on the Alaskan landscape is the alder. The tree homesteads in poor soil where other trees can't grow and, like a pioneer, paves the way for others to follow. Alders transfer soil-enriching nitrogen from the air to the ground in much the same way that legumes do. Sitka alder *(Alnus sinuata)* can add fifty-five pounds of nitrogen per acre per year. As the pioneering alder fortifies the earth, other trees move in behind it.

Sitka, or slide, alder is infamous among hikers. Dense thickets of slide alder commonly grow on mountainsides prone to avalanche. The slim, springy trunks of "avalanche alder" often grow bent over from repeated avalanches or winter snow load, making the tangles a real pain to pass through. But alders do have plenty of redeeming qualities. Snowshoe hares, deer, grouse, chickadees, bees, and other animals benefit from the alder species' bark, buds, and pollen. For humans, the tree is medicine cabinet and more. Alder bark contains salicin, a natural substance chemically similar to salicylic acid, which is used to make commercial analgesics. Alaska Native peoples used various parts of the tree to treat tuberculosis, insect bites, diarrhea, and rheumatic fever.

> **Sitka alder can add fifty-five pounds of nitrogen per year per acre to the soil.**

Alaska's Athabascan Indians used red alder *(A. rubra)*—so called because it yields a red dye—to tint fishing nets and other items. Because of its oily smoke, red alder is also the wood of choice for smoking salmon.

In addition to Sitka and red alder, thinleaf alder *(A. tenuifolia)* and the shrubby mountain, or green, alder *(A. crispa)* are also found in Alaska. Sitka, red, and thinleaf alders have gray bark and serrated leaves; the bark of mountain alder may be reddish brown to gray. Among all the species, one alder species or another is found in nearly every part of the state except the Arctic Coast and Aleutian Islands.

See also ASPEN; BIRCH

ASPEN The clacking whisper of trembling aspen leaves is one of the most distinctive voices of the soft-spoken plant kingdom. Aspen leafstalks, or petioles, are flat like a ribbon and set at right angles to the roundish leaf, so the slightest breeze can set leaves fluttering and rattling against each other.

"Quakies," "quakers," or "popple," as they're called, are the most widely distributed tree species in North America; in Alaska, *Populus tremuloides* is found from the northernmost part of Southeast Alaska, near Haines, to Southcentral, and throughout Interior as far north as the south slope of the Brooks Range. Aspens grow near streams, in creek bottoms, in upland meadows, on mountainsides up to about three thousand feet, and at the edges of coniferous forests. Even though aspens might grow on sites that appear dry, their presence is an indication that groundwater can be found near the surface during at least part of the year. The fast-maturing trees have relatively smooth greenish white to grayish bark, marked by thick black scars and prominent black knots.

Aspens reproduce primarily by cloning. What look like separate trees clustered in a group are actually one parent with its sucker offshoots growing from one primary, underground, horizontal root. Because they are essentially the same tree, individual clone groups within an aspen grove change to the same color at the same time and lose their leaves more or less simultaneously.

Walking in an open aspen woodland on an autumn day when the glowing yellow leaves are shimmying and swishing is one of life's soothing pleasures. Pioneers were comforted by the trees as well; aspen bark contains a substance that was used as a quinine substitute.

Humans aren't the only ones who find well-being among the aspens. Ruffed grouse balance along low branches nibbling buds and leaves, while snowshoe hares and moose nibble twigs and bark. Aspen groves are one of the beaver's favorite neighborhoods; the busy rodents eat the bark and use the wood for construction of lodges and dams.

Aspens do produce seeds, but rarely grow from them—the tiny seeds (three million to the pound) have neither stored food nor protective coating, so remain viable only a short time. In addition, aspen trees are either male or female; since all the trees in one clone group are the same sex, chances for seed pollination are inhibited.

Unlike birch trees, which often grow in mixed-species woodlands, aspens are usually found growing in single-species stands. Paper birch (*Betula papyrifera*) is often confused with aspen, but is distinguished by its peeling bark. Some alder species (*Alnus* spp.) can also be mistaken for aspen, but the gray-barked alder has decidedly oval, not roundish, leaves.

See also ALDER; BIRCH

BANEBERRY "Bane" means poison, death, and destruction.
Appropriately enough, Alaska's only poisonous berry is called baneberry (*Actaea rubra*). Eating as few as six baneberries can cause dizziness, increased pulse, and stomach pains in healthy adults; as few as two berries can kill a child. Fortunately, accidental poisoning is unlikely for anyone with normal taste buds as the baneberry is spit-reflex bitter.

The attractive but dangerous plant is found in moist, shady areas, open woods, and dry slopes from Southeast around to the Kenai Peninsula, Kodiak Island, Bristol Bay, and hundreds of miles up the Yukon River. Growing one to three feet tall, the baneberry bush has compound, toothed leaves and tiny white flowers that form a spike-like cluster at the top of the stem. All parts of the plant are poisonous.

Baneberry

Also called "chinaberries," baneberries look somewhat like ceramic beads; they can be either red or white in color, and are less than ½ inch in diameter. A black, pupil-like dot gives the berry its other common name, "doll's eye."

Although no baneberry deaths have been reported in the

United States, children abroad have been fatally poisoned by European species. As with any wild plant, be sure of its identity before you eat it.

See also ELDERBERRY

BIRCH The word birch is thought to derive from the Sanskrit *bhurga,* meaning "a tree whose bark is used for writing." If you don't feel like writing, raise a glass of homesteader's birch beer, made from the paper birch's slightly sweet sap. If tree beer isn't your thing, skip the fermentation and sip the vitamin-rich liquid au naturel. Better yet, cook the sap down into syrup and pour liberally over sourdough pancakes. If you are stranded far from cabin and pancakes, the inner bark, or cambium, can be nibbled for emergency survival rations.

Various species of wildlife also appreciate edible parts of the paper birch. Redpolls and other small, year-round birds rely on birch seeds for winter food. Ruffed and sharptail grouse browse the buds. Moose, deer, mountain goats, and snowshoe hares eat the twigs and beavers and porcupines gnaw the cambium.

Alaska paper birch *(Betula papyrifera* var. *humilis)* is most common in Interior Alaska, where it often grows in mixed forests with white spruce. Another variety of paper birch *(B. papyrifera* var. *kenaica)* grows in Southcentral parts of the state and on the Alaska Peninsula. Paper birch is found in a variety of habitats. The tree grows best on warm slopes with moist, porous soils, but is also found after fires on north-facing slopes and poorly drained lowlands. (Aspen, another white-barked tree commonly found in the Interior, does not have peeling bark. Also, birch twigs have a gritty texture that distinguishes birch from aspen and alder.)

Even though it's continually peeling off in thin sheets, the bark of paper birch is highly resistant to weathering. Downed trees may rot away, leaving an intact tube of bark. When building sod-roofed cabins, people sometimes put durable birch-bark sheeting under the sod to provide some waterproofing.

Not all birch species are trees with white, peeling bark. Dwarf birch *(B. nana)* has shiny, reddish copper, nonpeeling bark. The dwarf birch is considered a shrub and is nearly as widespread throughout Alaska as the ubiquitous willow. Found from the Arctic region to the Alaska Peninsula, dwarf birch isn't picky about habitat and will grow in a variety of situations, from wet lowland muskeg to rocky alpine slopes. The ½-foot to 3-foot-tall spreading shrub has small, roundish, scalloped leaves.

See also ALDER; ASPEN; SPRUCE; WILLOW

BLACK COTTONWOOD   The cottony seeds of black cottonwood trees are released in such profusion they sometimes collect in fluffy drifts on the ground.

Found in the river valleys and lowlands of Southeast and Southcentral Alaska, *Populus trichocarpa* is the largest broad-leaved tree in the state, and the fastest-growing tree in North America. A cottonwood discovered in 1965 northwest of Haines in Southeast Alaska stood at 101 feet tall and measured 32½ feet around, setting a national record.

Not content to rely solely on their abundant seeds for reproduction, cottonwoods produce such high levels of rooting hormones that cut twigs planted in wet ground can take root and grow into trees; logs left outside in the rain often develop sprouts. Cottonwood branches, placed in containers with other plants, stimulate rooting, an effect similar to commercial additives for boosting plant growth.

The cottonwood's triangular leaves are dark, glossy green on top and silvery gray underneath. In a breeze, the trees flash green-gray with a leathery, tapping sound. The honeyed scent of the leaf bud is industrially extracted for use as a fragrance in cosmetics and medicines.

Although the wood is soft, the grayish, heavily fissured bark can be hard enough to cause sparks when cut with a chain saw. Native Alaskans fashioned slit-eyed sun goggles from the bark, which was also crafted into fishing floats. As do other members of the willow family, *P. trichocarpa* contains the aspirin-like compound salicin in its bark.

Moose, rabbits, and other animals browse the cottonwood's leaves, buds, and catkins, and great blue herons choose the broad-crowned trees in which to locate their nesting colonies.

BLADDERWRACK Bladderwrack (*Fucus* spp.) is nature's squishier—and infinitely more interesting—version of plastic packing bubbles. Found on rocks along Alaska's coasts from the Bering Sea and Aleutian Islands to Southeast, this commonly seen seaweed grows high enough in the tide zone to be regularly exposed to air, and to beachcombers. The thumb-sized bladders make "old man's firecrackers" easy to identify and tempting to step on for the satisfying pop they make.

Bladderwrack

Inside the bladders is a sticky liquid with properties similar to aloe vera. Tidepoolers who scrape their knees and elbows on barnacles can simply pop open a bladder and smear themselves with "rockweed" juice for a soothing ointment. The mucilaginous liniment is also used to treat corns and skin tumors, and has been reported to ease rheumatic pain. A brown alga, bladderwrack is also a nutritious edible containing trace minerals and protein, and can be eaten raw, stir-fried, or added to soups.

Small pits on the outside of the bladders produce the seaweed's male and female gametes, which are released as waves splash against them—a method of reproduction that has worked for 570 million years.

BLUEBERRY AND HUCKLEBERRY Berries are Alaska's gift to its people and animals: something to leave a sweet taste in the mouth before fall freezes over—and throughout the winter, for industrious humans who plan ahead. Alaska has about fifty berry species. The handful of blueberry species and couple of huckleberries are among the most widespread and welcome berries of all in Alaska's kitchens and camps.

Some people call blueberries "huckleberries" and vice versa, and unless it's a botany test, either will do. Both are members of the *Vaccinium* genus, and all varieties are edible. The huckleberry name is commonly reserved for the only red *Vaccinium* (*V. parvifolium*), but some people—including taxonomists—also count the blackish bog blueberry (*V. uliginosum microphyllum*) as a huckleberry.

The bog blueberry is the most widely distributed blueberry or huckleberry. The many-branched, eight- to sixteen-inch-tall shrub with small oval leaves is found in bogs, open forests, and tundra throughout the entire state, except for the extreme northern coastal plain. A fair source of vitamin C, bog blueberries are harvested in the fall by people in Northern, Interior, and Western Alaska, where Alaska's more succulent varieties don't grow. Before there were mason jars and freezer bags, there were blueberries in seal oil, and pickled fish and bearded seal with blueberries. A popular Native dessert called *akutuq* is made of oil or liquefied fat mixed with blueberries and sugar. Bears, ptarmigan, and grouse also eat the berries.

The early blueberry (*V. ovalifolium*) is found throughout the Southeast and Southcentral parts of the state, across the Alaska Peninsula, and into the Aleutian Islands. This is the blueberry of coastal forests, where the spreading shrub may grow to five feet tall and form nearly continuous cover in open parts of the forest. The early blueberry and the Alaska blueberry (*V. alaskaense*) are favored by residents of Southeast and Southcentral for jellies, jams, liqueur, and freezer stocks. Blueberry leaves are also used for tea. The shrubs provide important winter browse for Sitka deer, mountain goats, and elk, and in summer, rufous hummingbirds feed on the nectar of the pink, quarter-inch-long, urn-shaped flowers.

Red huckleberry (*V. parvifolium*) is found only in Southeast. The three- to ten-foot-tall bushes grow along roadsides and in logged areas of forests. The berries are sour but flavorful, and are commonly used for jelly. Bears and blue grouse savor the sour berries, and huckleberry shrubs provide winter forage for Sitka black-tailed deer, elk, and mountain goats.

Where there are berries, there may be bears. Use caution when prospecting plentiful patches.

BROOMRAPE On the fringe of flower society, broomrape is among the 1 percent of flowering plants that are parasitic. Alaska's broomrape species, *Boschniakia rossica*, is parasitic on alder roots. Another broomrape species that preys on the broom plant gave this flower its name.

Also called ground-cone, broomrape looks like a cross between an upright spruce cone and a corn dog, pushing out of the soil through alder's leafy debris and standing sometimes up to a foot tall. (Chinese folklore has the plants springing from the semen of dragons or wild stallions.) Tiny oxblood-colored flowers crowd the stalk along with yellowish, scale-like leaves. Since broomrape takes its food from its host, it has no need to photosynthesize, and so no need for green leaves.

> Broomrape is among the 1 percent of flowering plants that are parasitic.

Broomrape is one of the few plants that have adapted to life on the ground in an alder thicket. The plant's parasitic (as opposed to photosynthetic) strategy for obtaining food is in response to the thicket's dense shade. And broomrape's stiff, upright shape keeps it from being buried under fallen leaves. Although not abundant, ground-cone can be found in alder thickets throughout most of Alaska, except the Arctic Coast and Aleutian Islands.

Bears commonly eat broomrape, although the plant is not widely eaten by humans. The white inner portion of the plant is, however, sometimes carved for use as a pipe.

See also ALDER

BULL KELP Like a harem of willowy sprites, bull kelp floats languidly upon the sea. At least, that's what it must have looked like to whoever assigned bull kelp's scientific name, *Nereocystis luetkeana*. *Nereo* is the Greek word for "sea nymph."

The fastest-growing of all seaweeds, bull kelp may reach lengths of two hundred feet in a year, growing in spurts of up to two feet a day. Anchored to a submerged rock below tide line by

its fist-like "holdfast,"
the ropy stipe grows
until the kelp's hollow,
tennis ball–sized, air-
filled bulb head floats
on the water's surface. Growing
from a "headphone" or "ear
muff" line across the bulb are
ribbony fronds ten to thirty feet long—
the mane of the sea nymphs.

Bull kelp

Large kelp beds, sometimes covering
many acres, are most common along Alaska's
outer coast from Southeast to the Aleutian
Islands. Extensive kelp beds can be hazardous for
boaters, but the same matted mass provides protective habitat for fish and marine invertebrates, and is a
haven to sea otters, who anchor themselves in the kelp
beds to keep from drifting while they sleep or eat.

In the hands of children (and some adults) the
long, hollow stipes of bull kelp cast up on beaches become
bull whips, cracked with glee and shouts of "Yaaa!" A more deco-
rous use for the sea vegetable is food; the hollow heads were a
traditional Native container for fish oil, and can also be stuffed
and baked. Kelp pickles are also popular. Only freshly harvested
kelp that is cut from its holdfast should be eaten, although
beachcombed kelp makes great garden mulch. Kelp extracts are
widely used in industry as thickeners and stabilizers.

BUNCHBERRY Bunchberries are dogwoods that decided
not to grow up. Most other members of the *Cornus* genus are trees
or shrubs, but *C. canadensis* rarely grows over six inches tall.
Looking like dogwood blossoms strewn on the ground in spring,
the four white "petals" are actually modified leaves, while round,
yellowish green knobs in the center are the real flowers. These
knobs develop into reddish orange berry-like fruits in late summer. According to one Pacific Northwest Coast Native legend, the
plants arose from the blood of a woman stranded high in a cedar

tree by her jealous husband. A bunchberry grew wherever a drop of her blood fell on the ground.

From central Alaska southward, bunchberries grow in muskeg and alpine areas and in the moist soils of woodlands and forests. The plants can form extensive beds by sending out underground stems.

Bunchberries are eaten raw with seal oil, or cooked with other berries. The fruits are mealy, but were nevertheless a staple for many Alaska Native peoples, who stored them in water and grease to eat throughout the winter. High in pectin and therefore useful as a thickening agent, bunchberry is also called "pudding berry."

These miniature dogwoods are important food sources for wildlife. Grouse and other birds eat the fruits, and in Southeast, bunchberry plants living in the forest stay green year-round, even under the snow, providing critical nutrition for deer and other animals. In more northern parts of Alaska, the leaves turn red and are shed in the fall.

BURL Burls are roundish, woody, wart-like growths commonly seen on the trunks of spruce and birch trees throughout Alaska. The largest of these tree tumors are sawed into slabs and fashioned into slickly varnished coffee tables and wall clocks. Whole trunks or limbs with burls are used as decorative posts, beams, or porch rails—cabin haute couture on the frozen frontier. The interior decoration of an Alaskan home seems incomplete without at least one burl something.

The growths begin as galls caused by fungi, insects, or bacteria. Burls grow markedly faster than their host tree, in somewhat the same way some human cancers grow. Although burls don't kill trees outright, they do weaken them, leaving trees vulnerable to disease or weather stress that might then kill them.

Trees with burls seem to occur in clusters, often in areas where it isn't easy to be

> Burls are growths that begin as galls caused by fungi, insects, or bacteria.

a tree, such as on the north side of a slope, on a wind-battered rocky shoreline, or near the latitudinal or elevational limit that trees can grow.

CEDAR Alaska yellow-cedar is the respected elder of Alaska's southern coastal forests. Probably the longest-lived of any Northwest tree, some Alaska yellow-cedars survive a millennium and more, growing to heights of eighty to one hundred feet.

Both of Alaska's cedar-like trees—the Alaska yellow-cedar *(Chamaecyparis nootkatensis)* and western red-cedar *(Thuja plicata)*—are actually members of the cypress family. (Most foresters use a hyphen in common names that are taxonomically misleading.)

Yellow-cedar grows throughout Southeast and north into Southcentral as far as Prince William Sound; red-cedar is found only in southern Southeast. In both species, needles look like tiny, yellowish green, flattened braids, and the outer bark is shredded and stringy. Cedars are usually free of lichens and fungi because the bark is too acidic for them. Cedar bark—especially the bark of yellow-cedar—was soaked, pounded, and woven into mats, clothing, and ropes. The Chilkat peoples incorporated cedar bark into their famous Chilkat blankets, which were woven of mountain goat hair and worn as ceremonial dancing robes by both men and women.

Even though other evergreens such as spruce and hemlock were far more plentiful in Alaska's coastal forests, the straight-grained, fine-textured, lightweight, durable, easily worked, rot-resistant, fragrant yellow- and red-cedar were the wood of choice for Native craftsmen carving canoes and totem poles.

Today, cedar is still used by Natives, and non-Natives as well, to create artwork and boats. The trees are also logged and used for structures, furniture, utility poles, cabinets, and pulp.

See also FOREST; HEMLOCK; SPRUCE

CHOCOLATE LILY Like a beauty queen who doesn't wash, the chocolate lily *(Fritillaria camschatcensis)* is lovely, even though it smells like a barnyard. The nodding, bell-shaped flowers grow on slender stalks, sometimes up to two feet tall. Also called black lily and Indian rice, this variegated brown to purple-black flower is Alaska's only *Fritillaria*—a kind of mottled or checkered lily.

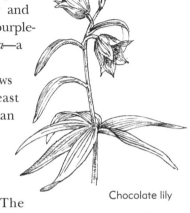

Chocolate lily

Commonly found in meadows along Alaska's coast from Southeast and Southcentral to the Aleutian Islands, chocolate lily bulbs were an important food for regional Native peoples, who pounded the bulbs into flour or dried them for later use in fish and meat stews. The chocolate lily's bulb forms a cluster of rice-like bulblets. When white explorers brought rice to Alaska, Haida people called it a name that meant "fritillary teeth." Traditionally, women harvested bulbs in the fall while the men were hunting geese. Bulb designs were incorporated into woven baskets and cedar boxes.

Chocolate lily bulbs are also favored by small rodents; voles harvest and store the food in underground caches.

COTTON GRASS No, that's not a derailed trainload of cotton balls strewn across the landscape—it's Alaska cotton grass (*Eriophorum* spp.). The one- to two-foot-tall sedge is found in tundra bogs, marshes, and wet roadsides throughout Alaska. Depending upon the species, cotton grass can have two to a dozen nodding, fluffy white heads on a single slender stalk. The "cotton" is actually the modified sepals and petals of tiny flowers.

Cotton grass has long been an important forage food for Alaska Native peoples. In early summer, the sweet-tasting rootstock is peeled and eaten raw. In the fall, mice collect the rootstocks, called "mousenuts," and cache them underground. Some Native children hunt for the stashes before the ground freezes, raiding the sweet root—sometimes leaving behind a substitute food for the mouse. When cut open, mousenuts resemble coconut meat. The Inupiaq peoples preserve mousenuts in seal oil for winter treats.

COW PARSNIP Neither poison ivy nor poison oak grows in Alaska, but that doesn't mean one can thrash about in the woods with impunity. The sap and outer plant hairs of cow parsnip *(Heracleum lanatum)* contain the chemical furanocoumarin, which can make skin extremely sensitive to sunlight. When skin that has come into contact with plant juices is exposed to the sun, a severe "sunburn" can result—complete with redness, blisters, and running sores.

Cow parsnip thrives in meadows and open woods from Interior Alaska through Southeast. The plant is hard to miss, as it can grow up to nine feet tall, with maple-like leaves as big as baseball gloves. Several parasol-shaped white flower clusters appear near the top of each plant. The thick, hairy stems are hollow. Cow parsnip looks quite similar to a couple of other dangerous plants, poison hemlock *(Cicuta mackenzieana)* and water hemlock *(C. douglasii)*.

Despite its skin-irritating properties, parts of the cow parsnip plant (which is also called "wild celery") are actually edible and have medicinal value. Stems can be peeled and eaten raw or cooked—with caution, as some individuals may be highly allergic to the plant. Aleut peoples drink cow parsnip tea to soothe colds and sore throats, and make compresses out of heated leaves to treat minor wounds and sore muscles.

True to the name, cows do browse on the leaves of this plant. Moose forage the dead leaves in winter, and bears and Sitka black-tailed deer nibble fresh shoots in the spring. Wild animals are reported to roll in the roots of cow parsnip when wounded, although dogs who roll in aboveground parts of the plant may lose patches of hair and develop red sores.

CRANBERRY Alaska has three species of cranberries: highbush, lowbush, and bog—all as crimson as the cheeks of cold children, all to be relished. Birds and bears eat the tart fruits as they are, but humans prefer their cranberries sweetened in nut breads, jellies, and jams. Long before New England Pilgrims began shipping Eastern species of cranberries back across the

Lowbush cranberry

Atlantic, Alaska Native peoples were gathering the berries and drying the fruits for winter food. Lowbush cranberries, also called lingonberries, contain the natural preservative benzoic acid, so they store well for several months.

Not just good to eat, Alaska's cranberries are wilderness medicinal plants. Highbush cranberry, also called "crampbark," possesses muscle-relaxing qualities. Some Alaska Native peoples brew highbush teas to treat stomach trouble. The Inupiaq apply a poultice of lowbush cranberries to soothe sore throats and rashes.

Lowbush cranberry *(Vaccinium vitis-idaea)* may be Alaska's most widespread single shrub species—found in forests, bogs, tundra, and alpine zones of every area of the state. The evergreen shrub grows only two to six inches tall and has shiny, oval leaves about three-quarters of an inch long. Lowbush cranberries are made into jams, jellies, relishes, and beverages.

Highbush cranberries *(Viburnum edule)* are deciduous shrubs from two to twelve feet tall and can be almost tree-like, with slender branches and leaves up to four inches long. Also called mooseberry, highbush cranberries are found in thickets, open forests, and streamsides of Southeast, Southcentral, the Alaska Peninsula, and the Interior. Alaskan and Northwest gardeners interested in landscaping with native species plant this shrub for its white flowers, pleasing foliage, and attractive red fruits, which draw birds and other wildlife.

Bog cranberries (referenced as both *Oxycoccus microcarpus* and *Vaccinium oxycoccus*) grow in sphagnum bogs and peat hummocks in coastal and northern forests throughout the state, except the extreme northern coast. The slender-stemmed evergreen

Highbush cranberry

creeps like a vine and grows close to the ground. This cranberry is seldom found in any abundance, and because it's so small is often overlooked altogether until the fall, when its berries glow red.

See also BLUEBERRY AND HUCKLEBERRY

CROWBERRY
Crowberries persist on their evergreen shrubs throughout the winter, creating a valuable cold-weather food supply for both humans and wildlife. People gather the crow-colored fruits from under the snow, as do grouse and ptarmigan.

Found in every single area of the state except a small slice of the Arctic Coast, crowberries *(Empetrum nigrum)* grow in arctic-alpine tundra, on moist rocky slopes, in muskeg, forests, and even on the rocky cliffs and nunataks of the Juneau Icefield. The heather-like shrub grows only about six inches tall and has short, blunt, needle-like leaves.

The juicy, pea-sized berries, also called blackberries by Alaskans, taste better cooked than raw, especially when mixed with more flavorful ingredients. Inupiaq people blend crow-berries with the livers of cod or trout into a dish called *tingaulik*.

See also NUNATAK

Devil's club

DEVIL'S CLUB
Rising on three- to ten-foot-tall canes bristling with sharp spines, devil's club is a bushwhacker's night-mare. Even the under-sides of the thorny plant's fourteen-inch leaves sport the stickers, which contain an irritant that can cause festering wounds.

But there are deals to be made with this not-so-completely-nasty devil. Devil's club *(Oplopanax horridus)* is a member of the ginseng family and has long been used by Alaska Native peoples for medicinal and shamanistic purposes. Tlingit and Haida peoples drank infusions of the bark for general health and applied devil's club bark poultices on wounds to reduce pain and swelling. Juice of the devil's club plant was also used in conjunction with dips in icy water for ritual cleansings. Some shamans wore necklaces of the plant's root laced with spruce and constructed purification shelters made of devil's club stalks.

Bears make use of Alaska ginseng as well. In Tlingit legend, it is said that shamans were first drawn to devil's club when they observed bears wallowing in the roots to find relief from wounds. Bears also eat the plant's scarlet berries, which grow in long clusters. In the autumn, leaves turn a lovely yellow gold and fall off, exposing a hedge from hell.

DIAMOND WILLOW

You'll most likely come across diamond willow inside city gift shops—perhaps in the form of a lamp stand or a walking stick made from creamy white wood marked with reddish, diamond-shaped depressions.

Diamond willow isn't a species of willow; it's the result of what *happens* to a species of willow, most commonly the Bebb willow *(Salix bebbiana)*, although a few other species are also susceptible. When a fungus—possibly *Valsa sordida*—attacks a willow branch, the branch dies back to the trunk. The fungus also kills the adjacent bark on the trunk and the layer of white sapwood where the affected branch joined the tree. The fungus doesn't, however, kill the red heartwood layer under the white sapwood, nor does the fungus kill the tree. The scar where the branch once grew is the diamond. In heavily infected trees, diamonds may touch each other, creating interesting patterns.

> Diamond willow isn't a species of willow, but a scar pattern left by a fungus attack.

In Alaska, diamond willow can be found from the Kenai Peninsula northward, most often growing in valley bottoms where vegetation is dense and sites are shady. The Copper River area may have the diamond willow mother lode—newel posts and balusters of the staircase at the Copper Center roadhouse are made entirely of the fungus-carved wood.

ELDERBERRY Raven went up along the river and came upon Stone and Elderberry quarreling over who should give birth to the Tsimshian people. Stone argued that if she were first, people would live a very, very long time. If Elderberry bore the first people, Stone claimed, life would be fleeting. Raven saw that Stone was about to deliver, so he touched Elderberry and told her to go first, which she did. And that is why people don't live as long as stones.

A glass of elderberry wine may seem in order after such a melancholy story. Blue elderberry and Old World black elderberry, found in Europe, are actually favored for wine making. But even though only the red elderberry *(Sambucus racemosa)* grows in Alaska, it is nevertheless transformed into jelly, tea, syrup—and Alaska's version of elderberry wine. (Although the pulp of the berry is edible if cooked, the stem pith, roots, leaves, and seeds contain hydrocyanic acid, which can cause diarrhea and vomiting if ingested.)

Red elderberry, or elder, grows as a shrub, 3½ to 14 feet tall with elliptical leaves. The red berries are preceded by dense, creamy white flower clusters, which inspire the nickname "Alaska lilac." This member of the honeysuckle family is native to the open woods and subalpine meadows of Southeast and Southcentral Alaska and into the Aleutian Islands.

FIREWEED Alaskans keep a watchful eye on fireweed throughout the short northern summer. *Epilobium angustifolium* grows a spirelike cluster of purple to magenta flowers that bloom from the bottom up. By the time the top buds blossom, summer is on the wane. When the seed pods begin to release their downy charges, the first snows can't be far behind.

Fireweed grows throughout Alaska and is especially abundant on the disturbed soils of avalanche tracks, gravel bars, burn areas,

clear-cuts, vacant urban lots, and mine tailings—
thriving in poor soils and areas ravaged by natural
and human forces. Often found in dense patches,
the two- to seven-foot-tall plant has erect stems
and willow-like leaves.

The entire plant is edible. Alaska Natives
peeled and ate the stems raw for the sweetish
pith; young shoots and leaves were collected
for greens, sometimes served with seal oil.
Contemporary users add fireweed flowers
to salads and gelatins. Bees are attracted
to fireweed too, and make delicious honey from the flowers.

A second member of this
genus, *E. latifolium,* is called dwarf
fireweed. "River beauty," as this plant is
more aptly called, is found on gravel bars
and riverbanks all across Alaska.

Fireweed

River beauty grows in patches, even in the poorest soil. The
plant is generally under a foot tall, with long, slender leaves.
Flowers are most commonly a bright magenta and much showier
than fireweed blossoms. In fact, another name for this member
of the primrose family is "rock rose."

Like fireweed, river beauty is also edible from flower to root.
Many Native Alaskans traditionally picked the plant before it
flowered to eat as fresh greens. They also enjoyed eating the
sweet pith as a treat.

Food is not the only use for this plant: stem fibers were
once woven into twine for nets and other purposes, and early
explorers reportedly found the downy seeds made an excellent
fire starter.

FORGET-ME-NOT A tiny yellow sun set in a summer
blue sky . . . how could anyone forget Alaska's official state flower?
Forget-me-not's tiny, yellow-centered blossoms bloom profusely
on fuzzy stalks up to eighteen inches tall with fuzzy, lance-shaped
leaves. The genus name, *Myosotis,* comes from the Greek for

"mouse ears," a reference to the plant's furry leaves. (Botanists use both *Myosotis alpestris* and *M. sylvatica* to refer to this species.)

Forget-me-nots thrive in meadows and along streams throughout much of the state. An arctic species of forget-me-not, *Eritrichium aretioides* (*E. nanum* to some botanists) has similar flowers, but grows in a four-inch-tall cushiony mat close to the ground on gravelly soils in the northern parts of the state.

HEMLOCK More than 70 percent of the trees in Southeast's dense coastal rain forests are hemlocks, distinguished by their thin, graceful branches and nodding tops. Hemlock needles are blunt and relatively soft; cones are only one to two inches long and appear purplish when immature. Alaska has two hemlock species, both of which grow throughout Southeast and parts of Southcentral.

The western hemlock *(Tsuga heterophylla)* is the larger of the two. Growing on moist flats and lower-elevation slopes, western hemlock may reach heights of 150 feet, with a trunk diameter of 4 feet. Mountain hemlock *(T. mertensiana)* is usually between 50 and 100 feet tall, with a ten-inch to thirty-inch trunk diameter. As indicated by its name, this hemlock grows not only at sea level, but is found up to an altitude of about 3,500 feet—higher than other conifers. Toward timberline, the mountain hemlock can take the form of a prostrate shrub.

> **Western hemlock may reach heights of 150 feet, with a trunk diameter of 4 feet.**

Some Alaska Native peoples ate the hemlock's inner bark, wrapped in skunk cabbage leaves and cooked in buried pits. The deeply furrowed outer bark yields tannin, which could be used for tanning hides.

Hemlock, along with Sitka spruce, comprises most of the timber harvested in Alaska for domestic and export markets. The wood is primarily processed into pulp and paper, although lumber from the trees is also made into boards, railroad ties, marine pilings, boxes, cabinets, and plywood veneer.

See also FOREST; SPRUCE

HORSETAIL This is the perfect plant for the harried parent who needs to both wash dishes in a creek and entertain a child in the wilderness. While the youngster is occupied popping apart and reconnecting the plant's jointed stems, the parent can scrub pots with this versatile, ancient plant called "horsetail" for its looks, "puzzlegrass" for its interlocking stem segments, and "scouring rush" for its traditional use in cleaning and polishing. In the New World, Native peoples used the gritty, silica-studded stalks to smooth arrow shafts, while in the Old World, knights used the same plant to polish their armor. Scouring rush is compared to the finest grades of steel wool.

Horsetail—among the oldest of all plants living today—is found throughout Alaska, growing nearly anywhere the ground is moist. Like ferns, these living fossils are relics from the time hundreds of millions of years ago when plants reproduced from spores, before seed-producing plants took over. The one- to two-foot-tall *Equisetum arvense* sprouts out of the ground looking somewhat like stalks of asparagus; spores are produced in the head. Some Native peoples considered new, still-tender shoots of spring a delicacy. Branches, which resemble long, soft pine needles, emerge in whorls around the jointed stem, making the mature plant look like a bottle brush.

INDIAN POTATO An Air Force survival publication points out what northern and interior Alaska Natives have always known: Indian potato is one of the most nutritious wild plants in Alaska. This pea-family plant is called *k'tl'ila*, "rope," by Athabascan people, an apt description since Indian potato roots can be two feet long. *Hedysarum alpinum*—also called Eskimo potato, Alaska carrot, and licorice root—stores well; Indian potato roots roots are sweetest in spring or fall and can be eaten raw or cooked. Kobuk River people crushed the root and used it as butter.

Indian potato roots

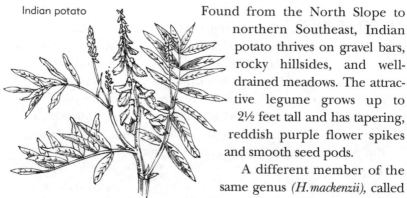

Indian potato

Found from the North Slope to northern Southeast, Indian potato thrives on gravel bars, rocky hillsides, and well-drained meadows. The attractive legume grows up to 2½ feet tall and has tapering, reddish purple flower spikes and smooth seed pods.

A different member of the same genus *(H.mackenzii)*, called "bear root "or "wild sweetpea," is believed to be toxic to humans. The Athabascans called this plant *ggagga k'tl'ila,* meaning "good food for bears." Bear root and Indian potato can be found in the same habitats in the same range, and are very similar in appearance. Native people who rely on Indian potato as a food source can tell the difference between it and bear root by looking at the taproot.

KINNIKINNICK Due to its hardiness and its ornamental appearance, you're as likely to see kinnikinnick in a highway median as in a forest or on the tundra. Found throughout the state in a wide variety of natural habitats, *Arctostaphylos uva-ursi* is also widely planted in commercial landscapes and suburban rockeries of Alaska and the Pacific Northwest.

An evergreen member of the heath family, kinnikinnick is a creeping, low shrub rarely over six inches tall, but sometimes spreading several yards in diameter. Trailing, matted stems have smooth red to purple bark, and the oval leaves are a leathery, deep evergreen. Waxy, urn-shaped flowers are white or pink, and berries are a dull orange-red. While the edible fruits are rather tasteless to humans, bears and spruce grouse forage for them; kinnikinnick's species name, *uva-ursi,* means "grape of the bear."

Native peoples did make tea from the leaves, but more often they smoked them. Confusion surrounds the origin of the name, but it seems likely that *kinnikinnick* is an Algonquin Indian word—meaning "smoking mixture"—carried north by explorers and trappers. Hudson Bay Company clerks and fur traders mixed kinnikinnick leaves with tobacco to extend their smoking supplies.

LABRADOR TEA The aromatic leaves of this shrub are shaped like long, thin, leathery fingers, perhaps resembling the tough fingers of Native traders and fur trappers who regularly gathered them to make tea. *Ledum decumbens* has several common names, all of which refer to where the plant grows and how (and by whom) it's consumed: "marsh tea," "Hudson Bay tea," "trapper's tea"—Labrador tea.

Common across the north country from Alaska to Greenland, *Ledum* spp. has a long history of human use. Athabascan Indians drank Labrador tea to ease the symptoms of heartburn and colds, and occasionally soaked bear meat in it to improve the meat's flavor. Yupik peoples drank the tea as a remedy for food poisoning and stomachaches. During the Revolutionary War, Americans chose to drink Labrador home brew instead of the king's tea. Fur traders and trappers also found some comfort in the beverage as an inexpensive and accessible substitute for black tea.

Circumpolar in its distribution, *L. decumbens* grows in muskegs, bogs, and forests throughout Alaska, except in Southeast. A second, closely related, species, *L. groenlandicum*, grows in marshes of Southeast and the Interior. Tea is made from the leaves of both species.

An evergreen shrub from six inches to three feet tall, Labrador tea is quite distinctive-looking with narrow leathery leaves that roll under around the edges. Even with its beautiful clusters of white flowers, this plant has the look of being tough enough to live under extreme conditions.

A light brewing of *Ledum* leaves makes a nice tea, but heavy-duty boiling can cause trouble. Oddly enough, all *Ledum* species contain ledol, a toxin that can cause dizziness,

Labrador tea

delirium, cramps, paralysis, and possibly death when taken in excess. Prolonged cooking releases large, potentially dangerous amounts of the chemical.

LICHEN In habitats with a variety of trees, shrubs, and plants, lichens often go unnoticed, or at most seem a subtle decoration. But in far northern environments where soils are poor, trees are stunted or nonexistent, and a less diverse, more inconspicuous array of plant species grows, lichens come into their own. On Alaska's northern tundra, lichens are significant, and sometimes dominant, components of the ecosystem.

Lichens are well suited to the northern environment because they don't require soil and can withstand extreme cold temperatures and dry conditions. All they need to grow is a little humidity and temperatures around 14°F. When conditions remain much colder than that, lichens simply lie dormant. In the Far North, lichens are extremely slow-growing. Once grazed over by tundra animals, lichens may take more than thirty years to grow anew. Some biologists speculate that the regeneration rate of lichens is related to the caribou's fifty- to one-hundred-year population cycles.

In fact, a lichen is not a single organism, but is an association formed between a fungus and an alga. The fungus, which has been described as "farming" the alga, provides the lichen's physical structure or platform, and also channels in moisture from the environment. The alga, supported within the fungus, performs photosynthesis to produce food, which it exchanges with the fungus for water and minerals.

Since lichens get their nutrients and water primarily from the air instead of the soil, they are very sensitive to air pollution. So sensitive that scientists monitored lichens to track the spread of radioactivity after the 1986 Chernobyl nuclear accident. The Nuclear Test Ban Treaty of 1963 came about in part because scientists found that radioactive material concentrated in lichen tissue; elements from nuclear fallout entered the human food chain through lichens, which were eaten by caribou, which were in turn eaten by people.

One of the most abundant and familiar of the Northland lichens is reindeer moss (*Cladina* spp.). Despite the name, it's not a moss, though reindeer and caribou indeed favor this greenish gray lichen. The reindeer reference also describes the two- to four-inch-tall, many-branched fruticose lichen, which looks somewhat like a jumbled mass of minuscule caribou antlers.

> Lichens don't require soil to grow and can withstand extreme cold.

Covering vast expanses of arctic tundra, reindeer lichen (as we'll call it) grows on open ground and sometimes forms thick mats on muskeg. This and other lichens comprise a major form of arctic vegetation—an important food source for musk oxen and moose as well as reindeer and caribou. Humans tend to consume lichens primarily as a survival food, though some northern peoples enjoy a "salad-like" delicacy of partially digested lichens taken from the stomachs of caribou killed in the winter.

In a less dramatic use, green-dyed reindeer lichen is commonly fashioned into fake bushes and trees in architectural models.

See also MUSHROOM; MUSKEG

LUPINE Lupines add more than beauty to the Alaskan landscape. The roots of this bluish purple, pea-like plant, a member of the legume family, has nodules on its roots that contain bacteria that fix nitrogen in the soil. The lupine's soil-enriching ability is especially useful in alpine zones and in the Arctic, regions where soils are thin and water from rain and snowmelt leaches out minerals. Lupines are as tough and tolerant as they are attractive. They germinate readily in harsh climates and are able to grow under poor conditions. Ten-thousand-year-old arctic lupine seeds, found frozen in a lemming burrow, germinated within forty-eight hours of being planted.

Alaska has five lupine species. Two of the most common are the widespread and northerly ranging arctic lupine (*Lupinus arcticus*) and the Nootka lupine (*L. nootkatensis*), found primarily in the southern part of the state and the Aleutian Islands. Both species thrive on mountain slopes, roadsides, gravel bars, and meadows. The plant usually grows one to two feet tall, and is readily identified by its distinctive leaf formation wherein five to seven finger-like leaflets radiate from a common point. After a rain or heavy dew, this palmate leaf often cradles in its center point a fat, perfect drop of water. Flowers are in cob-like clusters called "racemes."

Most beauties have a dark side, and lupine is no exception. Closely related to locoweed, lupine can be toxic to livestock if eaten in extremely large quantities—although McNeil River brown bears are reported to eat the roots with no ill effect. Historical records of human consumption exist, but lupine eating isn't generally recommended.

MUSHROOM From north of the Arctic Circle to the rain forests of Southeast, hundreds of fungus species live long, quiet lives in the Great Land. Alaska has both poisonous and edible mushrooms; knowledgeable foragers collect and eat about eight different species. The safest to identify are shaggy manes (*Coprinus comatus*) and hedgehogs (*Dentinum repandum*, formerly known as *Hydnum repandum*), but other Alaska fungal edibles include black morels (*Morchella* spp.), king boletes (*Boletus edulis*), and tumble-balls (*Bovista plumbea*).

People aren't the only northern fungus foragers: red squirrels, flying squirrels, and other small rodents collect, stash, and eat certain mushrooms as a delectable source of B vitamins and minerals.

Shaggy manes, found in the Interior, Southeast, South-central, and Arctic regions of Alaska, look like big thumbs with peeling skin. The tawny brown, cylindrical caps of this gilled mushroom appear in summer and fall, and are generally from a few inches to about six inches tall, although they may occasion-ally grow to a foot high.

A trip to the wilderness isn't required to gather shaggy manes, members of the inky cap family, which are among the most common fungi found in urban and suburban areas. Shaggy manes sprout on lawns, in fields, along roadsides, and even in gardens or compost heaps. As delicate as they look, "tennis court bane," as this species is also called, are tough enought to push up through asphalt. Although they're edible, consumption of overmature shaggy manes can cause indigestion, and shags from the roadside may be contaminated with pollutants. Before collecting and consuming *any* mushroom, consult a good field guide or, better yet, seek advice from a collector or mycologist experienced in identifying local mushroom species.

Shaggy manes

Hedgehog mushrooms, also known as "pumpkin pigs," sprout in the fall, under or near spruce or other conifers in Southeast and Southcentral Alaska. The hedgehog is a "toothed" mushroom, bearing a multitude of soft, spine-like teeth on its underside instead of gills. The cap of this stalked, white to orange mushroom can be up to six inches across and may be flattish, slightly depressed, or wavy, with the edge rounded under. Considered a choice edible mushroom, "sweet tooth" mushrooms, as they're also called, are said to taste something like oysters.

Mushrooms are the fruiting bodies of fungi. (Not all fungus species fruit—molds and yeasts are examples of nonmushrooming fungi.) Fungi reproduce by releasing spores, which produce thread-like growths called hyphae. The hyphae grow and fuse with other hyphae into bundles called mycelia, from which mushrooms may eventually sprout. Although mushrooms themselves are short-lived, mycelia can survive for centuries; one acre of tundra alone can contain an estimated two tons of living fungi.

In a biological kingdom of their own, fungi are neither plant nor animal. Like animals, they don't produce their own food, and so must obtain carbohydrates from green plants, which do make their own food through photosynthesis. Animals simply hunt or gather their food, but fungi employ other strategies. Some, such as the honey mushroom *(Armillariella mellea)*, are parasitic, drawing their nutrients from living plants. Others, like the chicken, or "sulfur shelf," mushroom *(Laetiporus sulfureus)*, are saprophytic and obtain nutrients by decomposing dead wood and plant matter. Still other fungi combine with photosynthetic algae to form lichens.

The fourth strategy, pursued by mycorrhizal fungi, is perhaps the most interesting. The term "mycorrhizal" refers to the mutually beneficial relationship between plants and the hyphae of certain fungus species. More than 90 percent of trees and green plants have vital symbiotic relationships with mycorrhizal fungi, the fruiting bodies of which include chanterelles and truffles—among the most desired of edible mushrooms. In exchange for food, mycorrhizae provide their associate plants with minerals, nitrogen, and water; fungally influenced water exchange is so efficient that mycorrhizally linked conifers are twice as drought resistant as nonassociated trees. Mycorrhizae also protect the plant from disease by releasing antibiotic chemicals and by forming physical and chemical barriers around the plant's roots.

Because mycorrhizal hyphae form extensive networks through the soil from plant to plant, some researchers believe that resources can be shared among the plants. Seedlings might receive nutrients from stronger plants until they are more fully developed, and deep-rooted trees may provide water for their neighbors during dry spells.

See also LICHEN

ORCHID Something as beautiful as an orchid is bound to have a complicated personal life. If novelists or psychologists wrote about orchid relationships, they might be titled something like "The Fair and the Fungal" or "Fungi and the Flowers Who Love Them."

Alaska's fourteen or so species of orchids (family Orchidaceae) all have codependent relationships with fungi. In truth, orchids and fungi need each other to survive. Delicate threads of fungal tissue present in the soil penetrate the orchid to pump in water and nutrients. The relationship is so predestined that appropriate fungi must be present in the soil for an orchid seed to sprout. In return, the orchid feeds the fungi carbohydrates that it makes through photosynthesis.

Orchids living happily ever after with Alaskan fungi include two species of lady's slipper, a fairy slipper (or calypso), a moccasin flower, one ladies' tresses, three bog orchids, two coral roots, and one each of fly-specked, rose-purple, twayblade, and Alaska rein. Some, like the lady's slippers, are easily recognized as orchids: the lower petal—markedly different from the other two—is enlarged into a pronounced, pouty "lip." Other orchids, such as the Alaska rein, twayblade, and bog, require a closer look to identify. All are relatively small and delicate and, depending upon the species, can be found growing wild in Alaska's muskeg, meadows, and woods.

> Each orchid species relies on a certain insect or insects for pollination.

The lives of orchids are further complicated by additional relationships with insects. While fungi provide nutrients and water, each orchid species relies on a certain insect or insects for pollination. In some cases, pollen must be on the exact right spot on the exact right insect for pollination to be carried out.

While an orchid needs lots of servicing to survive, it also needs to be left alone. Orchids have become rare around population centers because people pick them or dig them up in a futile attempt to transplant the ephemeral beauty to their own flower gardens.

SALMONBERRY The origin of this berry's name is a source of debate. Some claim salmonberries look like little clusters of salmon eggs; others insist the berries are so named because they're the color of salmon flesh. Still others contend that the plant gets its name from the fact that people drank tea made of its leaves and roots to settle stomachs upset from eating too much salmon. In Chinook legend, Coyote was instructed to put this berry into the mouths of the salmon he caught in order to ensure continued good fishing.

Rubus spectabilis grows in moist soil in lowland forests, in clearings, and along streams from southern Southeast through Southcentral and on the Aleutian Chain. A similar-looking *Rubus* member, *R. chamaemorus*, which grows in bogs throughout most of the state, is sometimes called salmonberry in some areas, especially in Western Alaska, but is usually known as cloudberry or baked-apple berry.

Salmonberry bushes, which may or may not have prickers, grow up to seven feet tall, often forming dense thickets. The juicy, red to orange-gold, cup-shaped berries ripen in August. (Along with debate over the berry's name, controversy also swirls around which color variation tastes best.) Salmonberries are just one of Alaska's half dozen species that belong to the *Rubus* genus, which also counts raspberries among its members. A sampling of the others includes the thimbleberry (*R. parviflorus*), nagoonberry (*R. arcticus*), western black raspberry (*R. leucodermis*)— and even the good old American red raspberry (*R. idaeus*). All are edible, delicious, and greatly appreciated by humans and animals alike.

Some claim that salmonberries are so named because they're the color of salmon flesh.

Berries of the *Rubus* genus can be divided into blackberries and raspberries. A raspberry pulls off cleanly from the bush, leaving a cup-shaped berry; a blackberry pulls the stem tip (receptacle) off with it. You'll spend a lot of time in Alaska pulling off berries from their stem in search of a blackberry, though. There are no true blackberries in Alaska.

SERVICEBERRY The Pacific serviceberry is a treat for the eyes and nose as well as the taste buds. Its blue-black fruits are juicy and sweet, and showy white flower clusters waft a pure perfume of spring. In the fall, its deciduous leaves brighten the landscape with yellows and reds.

Depending on conditions, *Amelanchier florida* (*florida* means "many-flowered") can take the form of either a shrub or small tree, growing in open woods and dry slopes from Southeast to the Alaska Peninsula. Under any alias—Juneberry, sarviceberry, Indian pear—the plant is extremely hardy and can survive in a wide range of soils. The look-alike saskatoon serviceberry *(A. alnifolia)* is occasionally found in Alaska's Interior, but is much less common in the state.

Serviceberry was the common fruit ingredient of traditional pemmican, a calorie-dense provision made of ground or pounded meat kneaded into a paste with melted animal fat and dried berries. Birds and bears are also fond of the tasty serviceberry fruits, which leave seedy, purple evidence in their droppings.

Native peoples used the hard, fine-textured wood of the serviceberry tree to fashion hunting and fishing implements.

Although sized like a berry, the serviceberry fruit is more closely related to an apple. Known biologically as a "pome," these "false fruits" grow not just from a flower's ovary, but from the flower stalk as well.

SKUNK CABBAGE

Skunk cabbage is a hillbilly cousin of the calla lily. Both have a central flower spike robed by a showy, petal-like leaf—but where the calla lily imparts an air of elegance, the skunk cabbage emanates eau de polecat. Which is not to say the swamp-dwelling skunk cabbage is less interesting. On the contrary. That it lives in Alaska in the first place is notable—swamps aren't the first habitat one associates with the Northland. But boggy woods and wetlands abound in Southcentral and Southeast, providing a welcome home for *Lysichitum americanum.* The plant noses out of wet ground sometimes even before snow is completely melted, and by summer may have grown into a cluster of five-foot leaves surrounding a twenty-inch flower spike.

As for the smell, we only call it bad because our civilized brains and socialized senses tell us to. This is the way the plant intends to smell. Sweet-smelling flowers attract a certain class of pollinator, such as bees. But the skunk cabbage is pollinated by flies and beetles, who prefer a more industrial scent. Unsophisticated? Hardly. The skunk cabbage—which can live up to seventy years—varies its distinctive scent according to

> Skunk cabbage noses out of wet ground sometimes even before snow is completely melted.

air temperature in order to attract whichever insect would be active at the time of pollination.

Skunk cabbage contains calcium oxalate crystals that burn human lips and tongues, so this is not a common food plant for people—although in times of shortage some Alaska Natives did roast the roots and grind them into flour. The large leaves were also used to wrap fish for baking and to line berry baskets.

Animals seem to be able to eat skunk cabbage with no ill effect: bears dig up the rootstock, and Vancouver Canada geese and Sitka black-tailed deer browse the leaves.

SOAPBERRY "Whipped-cream berry" might be a more appropriate name for this plant. Soapberries *(Shepherida canadensis)* contain saponin, a nonsweet sugar derivative that causes the berry to lather when beaten. Northwest Coast Native peoples whipped the bitter-tasting soapberries with fish oil (usually the oil of eulachon), sugar, and water to make "Indian ice cream." Much smaller quantities of saponins are also found in beets and green tea; in industry, saponins are used as foaming and emulsifying agents and detergents.

Soapberry bushes grow in open woods and dry slopes from the northern Interior to Southeast. They are hardy shrubs three to eight feet tall, with brownish, scaly, dry-looking leaves and stems; the oval leaves appear flocked. Brownish yellow flowers grow on both the male and female plants, but only the female plant produces the small, translucent, red-orange berries.

See also EULACHON

SPRUCE Three spruce sisters live in Alaska: Sitka spruce *(Picea sitchensis)*, white spruce *(P. glauca)*, and black spruce *(P. mariana)*.

Sitka spruce trees grow to awesome heights in their centuries-long lives, standing like exquisitely designed steeples among the more numerous nodding hemlocks of Southeast's coastal rain forests. Sitka spruce grow only in Southeast and Southcentral Alaska, where individual trees may reach heights of two hundred feet. Some groups of Alaska Native peoples considered this spruce to be the most important tree in the forest, possessed of a potent and benevolent spirit. The inner bark provided food, sap yielded healing balms, boughs made beds, lumber built boats, and roots were woven into baskets and nets.

Sitka spruce's little sisters, white and black spruce, don't grow in Southeast, but are widespread throughout the Interior.

White spruce, which grows fifty to sixty feet tall, is the most common tree in Interior Alaska, where it often grows intermixed with paper birch. Black spruce is a smaller tree. Because black spruce tolerates the poor, wet soil of muskeg and tundra, which are often underlain with permafrost, its growth may be stunted. Black spruce trees are often under ten feet. Under good conditions, black spruce can grow to about thirty feet.

Sitka and white spruce are among Alaska's most commercially important trees. White spruce is used extensively for construction in Interior Alaska and was sought after by earlier settlers, who used the wood to build log cabins and to construct flumes and sluice boxes for gold mining. The light, resonant wood of Sitka spruce is used to make guitars, pianos, boats, small planes, and gliders, and is also pulped for newsprint.

All spruces have papery cones and short needles that grow on all sides of the twig. Needles of the black and white spruce are four-sided and can be easily twirled between the fingers, but Sitka spruce needles are more flattened, with a slight keel, and not so easily rolled.

White spruce

See also BIRCH; FOREST; HEMLOCK; MUSKEG; PERMAFROST; TUNDRA

SUNDEW The sundew is a delicate-looking bog plant with an indelicate appetite for unsuspecting insects. Of the fifty or so insectivorous plants worldwide, Alaska has two: the roundleaved sundew *(Drosera rotundifolia)* and the narrowleaf, or long-leaf, sundew *(D. anglica)*. Neither grows taller than a spool of thread, and both grow in wet meadows, in muskeg, and along the marshy fringes of ponds and rivers throughout most of the state except for the high Arctic.

Leaves of the roundleaved sundew look like tiny soupspoons fringed with red hairs that appear to be covered with dew. Narrowleaf leaves are shaped more like slightly cupped canoe paddles and are also covered by sticky hairs. Each species employs a different technique of lying in wait for passing prey: the roundleaved sundew holds its leaves near the ground and waits for spiders and other crawling insects to get caught in its gummy hairs; narrowleaf plants hold their leaves up, hoping to similarly snare low-flying insects.

> The roundleaved sundew waits for spiders to get caught in its gummy hairs.

When an insect gets stuck on the leaves, the hairs, which are really glands that secrete the dewy digestive juices, bend around the prey and begin digesting it.

Most green plants get by just fine on a straight diet of photosynthesized sunlight and soil nutrients. But bogs have notoriously poor, acidic soil, so the sundews' insect-eating strategy supplements its photosynthesis. Energy derived from the extra nutrients may be applied exclusively to producing seeds.

TAMARACK Perhaps in sympathy with the aspens, tamaracks let their needles go gold and fall off each autumn. During winter the bare little conifers may look dead, but they're simply biding their time. Come spring, *Larix laricina* grows a new crop of tender, chartreuse-colored needles, much to the delight of the grouse, who have been eating tough spruce needles all winter.

In Alaska, the slow-growing trees, which top out at about fifty feet, are found only in the Interior, where they usually grow on boggy ground, often in the company of black spruce.

The tamarack is the only deciduous conifer that grows in Alaska (other deciduous conifers include species of cypress and redwood). Shedding needles is one way a tree can guard against drying out in severely cold, windy environments; bare branches also help protect the larches from storm damage.

Also called Eastern larch, Alaska larch, or hackmatack, the spindly tamarack has unexpectedly durable wood, which is utilized in making posts, poles, and railroad ties, and in framing houses.

WILD ROSE A rose is a rose is a rose—or an apple, strawberry, raspberry, mountain ash, cinquefoil, or any other of the three thousand species in one hundred genera in the huge Rosaceae family. Most members have roundly symmetrical flowers with five petals. Alaska has at least twenty-two native family members, four of which grow to small tree size: serviceberry, Oregon crabapple, Greene mountain ash, and Sitka mountain ash. But what really comes to mind when we say Alaska rose is the delicate, blushing wild rose.

Alaska has three thorny species of wild rose. The prickly rose *(Rosa acicularis)* can grow to six feet tall in woods, forests, roadsides, and bogs from the south slope of the Brooks Range throughout the state except Southeast, Kodiak Island, and the Aleutians. The Nootka rose *(R. nutkana)* can reach heights of eight feet and forms thickets along beaches in the coastal areas of Southeast, Kodiak Island, and parts of Southcentral. The third species, the Woods rose *(R. woodsii)*, named for an English botanist and rose specialist, may be an escaped cultivar and has been found only near Circle Hot Springs and Tok in Interior Alaska.

In Alaska, wild roses more often end up in canning jars than in vases. Their chickpea-sized fruits, called rose hips, are among the richest known food sources of vitamin C. Rose hips look like red, thick-skinned, fleshy berries with topknots. Three large hips have more vitamin C than an orange and also contain significant amounts of other vitamins and minerals. "Neechees," which retain their food value relatively well when dried, have saved many an Alaska Native and pioneer during times of famine. Grouse and other birds also rely on rose hips, which persist on the bushes throughout the winter.

Wild rose

The fruits are fairly bland on their own, but enhanced by other ingredients they make excellent jam, marmalade, even ketchup. Tea is brewed from rose leaves and petals, and moistened petals applied to small wounds serve as emergency Band-Aids. Rose petals in various forms of application are a time-honored treatment for dry or irritated skin.

Wild roses may look plain next to their cultivated kin, but the fragrant, five-petaled, rose pink flowers have the elusive, enchanting beauty reserved for wild things.

WILLOW Wherever you are in Alaska, you're never too far from the nearest willow. *Salix* spp. has adapted to life in every corner of the state, from the Arctic Coast to southern Southeast—and nearly all the islands, gravel bars, and talus slopes in between.

Of the world's three hundred or so willow species, about fifty-six are present in Alaska. Found in open forests, on stream banks, on tundra—and in nearly every other terrestrial habitat type, in nearly every nook and cranny of the state—willow takes many forms, from prostrate shrub to bush to tree. Most willows have slender leaves and slim twigs, and many have yellow to orange branches in the winter. But even individual trees within the same species can grow either as shrubs or trees and may have leaves that differ in size, shape, and texture from the the leaves of their same-species neighbor. To further foil attempts to identify the different willows, species hybridize easily and frequently.

Willows don't just take up space without giving anything in return. They serve as nature's hardware store, grocery store, and pharmacy. Native Alaskans twisted willow bark into twine for nets and fishing line, and the supple twigs of Sitka willow *(Salix sitchensis)* and other willow species are still used for weaving baskets and stretching hides.

Alaska Native peoples ate the peeled, fresh shoots and inner bark of feltleaf willow *(S. alaxensis)*—a species that occurs only in Alaska. The inner bark was also dried and ground into flour to make bannock, an unleavened bread. A wide variety of animals also depend on willow for food, including moose, deer, beaver, snowshoe hares, ptarmigan, and grouse.

Willow is an excellent source of vitamin C, and also contains significant amounts of salicin, a natural form of aspirin that was traditionally used as an anti-inflammatory. Salicin was listed in the official *United States Pharmacopoeia* until 1926. Northern Native peoples chewed fresh willow and applied the paste to insect stings to relieve pain and swelling.

In the spring, willow catkins lend a welcome, festive fuzziness to the season. Catkins, tassels of minute flowers, appear on willows and other Alaskan trees and shrubs, often before leaves come out. Catkins on the male willow plants produce pollen that are carried by wind to catkins on the female plant. Typically, male catkins are longer and more eye-catching than their female counterparts.

Catkins on the arctic willow *(S. arctica)* are specially adapted for the cold climate. The extremely hairy catkins of these low-growing shrubs help trap warmth near the plant, and specialized cells allow the flowers to withstand freezing temperatures. The catkins of some dwarf willow species have been known to resume growth after three weeks at temperatures as low as 14°F.

> **Willows are nature's hardware store, grocery store, and pharmacy.**

Only wind-pollinated plants form catkins. With no need to attract insects, flowers don't have to be showy or fragrant, but the pollen does have to be fine and dry in order to disperse well on the breeze.

Other Alaskan trees that form catkins include aspen, birch, and alder. Aspen and willow trees are segregated male or female, but birch and alder bear male and female catkins on the same tree—sometimes on the same twig.

See also DIAMOND WILLOW

WITCHES'-BROOM

Witches'-brooms are bushy growths seen in some of Alaska's trees. With a little imagination, they do indeed look like the end of a witch's broom—especially if she's used it more for sweeping and punching cobwebs than for riding.

In the Interior, white and black spruce produce the abnormal-looking tufts of small branches when the tree becomes infected with plant rust—a disease caused by fungi in the order Uredinales. The tufts may be mistaken for squirrel nests, which in fact they often become; northern flying squirrels favor witches'-broom for winter den sites.

The broomy mass is brown and dead-looking in the winter. In spring, if the broom is still alive, small yellow lesions appear on the broom's new needles; over the summer these pustules enlarge and turn bright orange or rust colored. A strong, sweet odor is often present—possibly explaining why porcupines are drawn to chew on affected branches. The matured lesions release countless spores, by which the fungus reproduces itself.

> Witches'-brooms don't kill their host tree, but they do weaken it.

Instead of infecting another spruce tree directly, the spores usually attack an intermediate host first, often a bearberry plant. Spores subsequently released off the plant will then invade a tree.

In Southeast Alaska, dwarf mistletoe (*Arceuthobium tsugense*) causes witches'-brooms to form, primarily in hemlock trees. When mistletoe grows on a hemlock branch, the parasite's roots spread below the bark to steal water and nutrients. As the mistletoe grows, hormones of the host branch are affected, sometimes altering the regular growth pattern into the tangled clump of a witches'-broom.

Witches'-brooms don't kill their host tree, but they do weaken it, making it more vulnerable to other diseases and weather-related stress.

WOOLLY LOUSEWORT Woolly
lousewort looks something like a stunted snapdragon emerging from a wispy cocoon. The silky overcoat, which provides a layer of insulation, is a smart adaptation for a plant that lives on Alaska's exposed tundra and alpine slopes. Found from the Arctic through Southeast, the six-inch-tall *Pedicularis lanata* is indeed a member of the snapdragon family. The "lousewort" tag derives from the old, incorrect superstition that live-stock grazing on *Pedicularis*, which translates as "little louse," became infested with lice.

Woolly lousewort

Around June, rose pink blossoms burst through the woolly protection. Each flower has a large lip for the landing convenience of bees—the primary lousewort pollinators. Leaves are fern-like.

The entire plant is edible and has been used traditionally by several Native groups. Inuit children are said to enjoy sucking the nectar from lousewort blossoms, and Inupiat peoples ferment the deep pink flowers, which may then be eaten with oil and sugar. Roots are eaten both raw and cooked.

YELLOW POND LILY Looking like sculpted butter,
the pond lily *(Nuphar polysepalum)*, also called Indian pond lily, floats lightly on shallow ponds, in slow streams, and at the edges of lakes from Southeast to the Brooks Range. The distinctive, bright yellow three-inch flowers and their foot-long, elongated heart-shaped leaves are anchored to the muddy bottom by spongy stalks. Moose bob for buried rootstock, one of their favorite foods. Beavers and muskrats cache the roots as a winter food supply.

The plant's rootstock and seeds were staple foods for Native peoples, particularly in the Pacific Northwest. Roots were boiled or roasted, and the seeds were ground into flour or toasted. Today's most resourceful Alaskans fry pond lily seeds to enjoy as nutritious mock popcorn.

THREE

Natural Features

YOUNG AND RESTLESS, Alaska is a soap opera of terrestrial turmoil. The land shifts, groans, grinds, erupts, freezes, thaws, burns, and bubbles over with earthquakes, glaciers, volcanoes, and general shrugging around. But this behavior is to be expected from a land cobbled together from colliding chunks of drifting earth.

The Great Land is a crazy quilt of continental crust; as many as fifty blocks are thought to have drifted together into the interlocked landform we now know as Alaska. The process has occurred in stages, the last one beginning about two hundred million years ago and still happening this very day. The most recently arriving piece is called the Yakutat block; sandwiched between the Pacific and North American tectonic plates, this transient chunk of crust is moving north along the Queen Charlotte–Fairweather fault system in Southeast Alaska. In its travels, the block has caused earthquakes along the coast and is responsible for lifting the St. Elias Mountains even higher—which seems like overkill, since a number of North America's highest peaks already roost in the Wrangell–St. Elias Range.

Not surprisingly, Alaska's geographic personality is formed in large part by the quirks of a geologically volatile land. The state claims more than eighty potentially active volcanoes and many more inactive ones. The greatest eruption anywhere on earth during this century happened in 1912 in what is now called Valley of Ten Thousand Smokes in Katmai National Park and Preserve on the Alaska Peninsula.

Alaska also was the scene of North America's strongest earthquake. The magnitude 9.2 Good Friday quake of 1964 devastated much of the Southcentral part of the state.

Hot springs are scattered from Southeast all the way to the arctic Brooks Range. Only about 17 of Alaska's 124 or so known hot springs have been developed in any way, and only a handful of those are accessible by road—even though more than eleven million acres have been identified as containing important geothermal resources.

The weather that passes over Alaska today is influenced by where and how all those chunks of continental crust came together. Several mountain ranges—born from crustal interactions—mark the boundaries of three of Alaska's four distinct climate zones: maritime, continental, and arctic (the fourth, the transition zone, is in Western Alaska).

Between the arctic zone in the north and the continental zone of the Interior, the Brooks Range checks harsh weather trying to blow south. In the maritime zone of Southcentral Alaska, the Alaska, Chugach, Wrangell, and Aleutian Ranges act to filter weather moving north, effectively drying the air before it reaches the Interior. Of course, many other factors also influence the weather—one of the most significant being Alaska's high-latitude address near the top of the globe.

The farther you get from the equator, the more dramatic seasonal change becomes. At the equator the sun is directly overhead, but because the earth is tilted a little bit in its rotation around the sun, the poles are always either leaning away from the sun or leaning toward it. So, the angle and the amount of sunlight striking northern (or southern) latitudes depend on where the earth is in its rotation. The Arctic Circle marks the latitude line where, on the day of the summer solstice, the sun doesn't set. On the flip side, Far North communities such as Barrow don't see the sun for two months in the winter.

Globally speaking, northern regions are cold because they simply receive less solar energy. Even in summer the sun strikes at a long angle. Imagine pointing a flashlight at a basketball. Held directly on the middle, the light is strong and powerful. But if you train the light across the top of the ball, that part of the light shining on the ball seems weak by comparison, since much of the light dissipates into space. The relative weakness of the sun falling on Alaska—at the top of the ball, so to speak—allows permafrost to stay frozen and creates a cool climate conducive to the growth and stability of glaciers. Glaciers are much more conspicuous than permafrost, but both features figure prominently in Alaska's geographic profile.

Giant waves and winds with names like taku and williwaw also work their forces on the Great Land; in the space of two centuries Alaska has had seven fatal tsunamis and the largest seiche (splash) wave ever recorded.

Sitting at the top of the globe seems to bring Alaska closer to the heavens, and sky watching can be a rewarding pursuit. Sun dogs appear at their stations flanking the sun, and sun pillars and circular rainbows called glories add flair to summer's endless daylight.

If twilight is your time, Alaska is your place. The sun is slow to rise and slow to set, resulting in a half-light that peers low across the landscape. Sunsets can linger for an hour, and in the northern part of the state a steady twilight replaces darkness from mid-May until late July. Of course, a few hours of twilight replace light in the northern winter.

But dark skies have their rewards. In the winter, luminescent northern lights hang like waving, celestial laundry or twirl green and pink in an atmospheric dance of the shining veils. People come from all over the world to witness the aurora, which on some endless winter nights fills the sky for hours.

Larger than Texas, California, and Montana combined, Alaska has plenty of room to warehouse its store of natural features. In the 2,400 miles from its western to eastern borders and the 1,420 miles north to south, a vast array of amazing sights can be seen on—and above—the landscape of the Last Frontier: sastrugis to sun dogs, nunataks to noctilucent clouds. And, of course, northern lights, which shine like neon WELCOME TO ALASKA signs on even the coldest, darkest nights.

ARCTIC CIRCLE While rivers run crooked and mountain ranges wander, we orderly humans scribe straight lines and perfect circles to designate earth's official sections. The Arctic Circle is such a line, crossing tundra, forest, and steppe like a headband around the northern part of the globe.

The circle's geographic address is 66°32 N, which just about puts it through the main street of Fort Yukon, 125 miles north of Fairbanks.

The Arctic Circle is actually an astronomical demarcation, marking the latitude of the midnight sun. At the Arctic Circle, the sun doesn't dip below the horizon on the day of the summer solstice (June 21 or 22) and doesn't rise above the horizon on the day of the winter solstice (December 21 or 22).

Even though the circle itself is imaginary, a sign alongside the Dalton Highway (the road to the Prudhoe Bay oil fields) marks the spot—a wonderful photo opportunity for geographic romantics.

ARCTIC OCEAN If you want to plant a flag at the North Pole, take an ice auger instead of a posthole digger. There is no land mass at the top of the globe, just the Arctic Ocean—the center of which is covered by a perpetual sheet of ice, ten to fifteen or more feet thick.

The Arctic Ocean covers the top of the globe with about 5.5 million square miles of water and ice. Even though it's only about 8.5 percent the size of the Pacific Ocean, the Arctic Ocean is still the fourth-largest ocean in the world. Its average depth is 5,010 feet, but depths of 17,880 feet have been measured.

Because great volumes of freshwater flow in from rivers in Alaska and Siberia, the Arctic Ocean has relatively low salinity, and so freezes readily; each winter, ice coverage increases by a third. Summer temperatures at the North Pole hover around freezing, and in winter may drop to −89°F. Despite these harsh conditions, the northernmost sea supports a rich diversity of life, from microscopic plankton to thirty-ton whales.

Survival strategies vary among year-round animal residents.

Polar invertebrates such as members of the shrimp and crab families tend to have higher concentrations of salt in their tissues to keep their body fluids flowing in the frigid water. And some vertebrate fishes withstand the cold by producing an antifreeze-like compound that keeps their tissues from freezing. Even this protection can fail, however, if the fish comes into direct contact with ice crystals, so most arctic fish spend much of their lives at lower depths where they're less likely to run into ice.

> The center of the Arctic Ocean is covered by a perpetual sheet of ice.

Although polar marine plants and cold-blooded animals are adapted to the cold, they can't tolerate rapid temperature changes. Fortunately for them, the major mass of Arctic Ocean water never alters more than a few degrees, even from winter to summer. Perhaps this explains why life under the ice seems to go on as normal all winter. In fact, some biologically critical annual events take place in the "dead" of winter. Arctic cod, for instance, spawn under the ice between November and February. Small, shrimp-like animals critical to the northern marine food chain also spawn under the ice in the winter months. Arctic kelp is known to experience a growth spurt in the winter, and algae and plankton are active as well.

Many warm-blooded mammals, including ringed seals, polar bears, and humans, have also adapted to polar conditions, opting to stay in the waters, on the ice, or on the Arctic Ocean shore through the long, cold winter.

See also HUMAN SETTLEMENT; POLAR BEAR; SEA ICE

BERINGIA (BERING LAND BRIDGE) About

seventy million years ago, Alaska and Siberia were connected by a low-lying plain that extended from Point Barrow south to the Pribilof Islands—a distance of hundreds of miles. Beringia, as geologists call it, was forested and cut with large rivers. About fifteen million years ago rising seas began to flood Beringia, which by about three million years ago was completely submerged. Since then, "land bridges" across the inundated territory have emerged

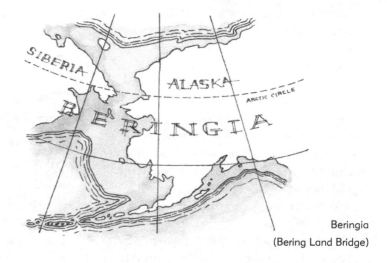

Beringia
(Bering Land Bridge)

and disappeared a number of times, the original forest replaced by grasses and shrubs. The bridges reappeared during periods of active glaciation, or ice ages, because more water was held in the glaciers, lowering sea levels. The world has experienced multiple ice ages of varying extent.

Before Beringia was first submerged, mammals had dispersed both ways between Asia and North America via the land bridge, but during the last two million years, dispersal was primarily from west to east, Siberia to North America, and included such animals as deer, lynx, early bears, horses, saber-toothed tigers, and hares.

During the last land-bridge migration opportunity, which ended about ten thousand years ago, more than twenty species made the eastward journey, including woolly mammoths, musk oxen, caribou, moose, bison—and human beings. Today, Alaska and the Siberia's Chukchi Peninsula are separated by the Bering Strait, only 56 miles wide at its narrowest point.

See also HUMAN SETTLEMENT

BREAKUP   Breaking up isn't so hard to do in Alaska. It happens on a yearly basis, in fact. "Breakup" is the unofficially recognized Alaska mini-season when river and sea ice breaks apart as temperatures warm and water levels rise. Breakup is also the time when Alaskans in the Interior and northern parts of the state begin to see puddles instead of sheets of ice; nothing says spring like standing water.

On large rivers such as the Yukon, breakup can be a spectacular show accompanied by booms, creaks, and groans as the frozen surface snaps apart and riverine icebergs push past—and sometimes over—each other.

Breakup is a mixed blessing. This harbinger of spring can result in huge ice jams that may cause flooding in nearby communities. Also, travel via frozen river grinds to a temporary halt; the ice is too unstable for snow machines and dogsleds, but it's still too early for boats. Before long, however, groaning bergs and slabs are replaced by shards and thin plates of ice tinkling pleasantly on the way downstream, and smiling sourdoughs tune up their outboards.

Since about 1916, Alaskans have enjoyed placing wagers in the Nenana Ice Classic betting pool on when the ice will "go out." Winners who guess the moment of breakup to the nearest minute split a pot usually worth more than $200,000. To mark the moment, a large wooden tripod rigged with a trip wire is erected on the frozen Tanana River at the town of Nenana. As soon as the tripod begins to move downstream, the wire breaks, stopping a clock on shore. The latest Ice Classic breakup date recorded was May 20, 1964; the two earliest was April 20, in 1940 and 1998. About 70 percent of breakups occur in May.

See also RIVER; SEA ICE

THE BUSH The term "bush" has more to do with a state of mind and a way of life than a kind of shrub. When Alaskans talk about the bush, they're usually referring to the more remote parts of the state accessible only by boat, small plane, dogsled, snow machine, or foot. Most people who live "Outside," as the rest of the United States is called, have to make an effort to find solitude, open space, and wilderness, but in Alaska, towns and villages are mere camps in a wild landscape; the majority of towns in Alaska aren't connected by roads.

There are bush towns, such as Kotzebue (population 3,237), and bush villages, like Nikolski (population 38), most of which have some form of electricity and running water. Trappers, homesteaders, and other single people or families living self-sufficient lifestyles, Natives and non-Natives alike, live in isolated cabins, sometimes with a generator for electricity and a well, sometimes with no electricity or running water. Outhouse construction is an art form in the bush.

Cabin fever can strike any Alaskan who has been forced indoors by cold and dark, but this feeling of bored restlessness (cabin fever has been described as "a twelve-foot stare in a ten-foot room") is especially heightened when there's no town to go to or people to talk to for a hundred miles.

Some bush residents, particularly those who live alone and have only infrequent contact with other people, may become idiosyncratic or eccentric and are sometimes said to have gone "bushy."

See also SAD

COAL Alaska is thought to hold about half of our country's coal resources, much of it buried in the North Slope. The logistics of mining and transporting coal in the frozen, roadless Far North have kept exploitation of this resource to a minimum. Alaska's one commercial coal mine, Usibelli Coal Mine, is located near what was once a tropical forest and what is now Denali National Park and Preserve. Sometime between the tropical forest days millions of years ago and the present, the area was flooded and many layers of sediment were laid down, beginning the slow road from green plant to coal plant.

Basically, coal is compressed ancient forest, and can trace its roots to plants that die in a wet, acidic environment. Instead of completely decaying, the plants only partly decompose, forming a soft, fibrous organic substance that we call peat (the same peat you buy in bales at the plant nursery). Over time, sediments are laid down over the peat, compressing and heating it, and pushing out most of the moisture. This compressed and heated peat creates a soft brown coal called lignite. If lignite is further compressed and dried, bituminous coal results. Coal in its final, hardest form is called anthracite. Anthracite is about 96 percent carbon and produces the most heat of the three types of coal.

Although some anthracite does occur in Alaska, most of the state's coal is bituminous or subbituminous grade. The Usibelli mineextracts about 1.5 million tons of coal each year. Typically, around half of that is exported to Korea, and half of which was exported to Korea and half of which was sold to such buyers as the University of Alaska, military bases, and Municipal Utilities Service of the Interior. These buyers use coal to power huge generators, which produce heat and power for residents; Alaskans don't typically burn coal in their homes. Maybe in a million years a few more mines will open: Alaska has an estimated twenty-seven million acres of peat, averaging seven feet thick.

COPPER In 1885, Athabascan chief Nikolai of Taral, a small village at the confluence of the Copper and Chitina Rivers in Southcentral Alaska, showed his personal copper deposits to a military explorer. A little over two decades later, the Kennicott Copper Mine opened for business near the banks of the Chitina River in the mountains of the Wrangell–St. Elias Range. Until it closed in 1938, Kennicott was the richest copper mine in the world—extracting ore worth about $1 billion at today's prices.

Copper had long been of particular value to the Northwest Coast peoples of Southeast Alaska.

Copper

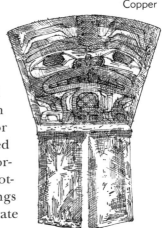

Pounded into flat, large, shield-shaped plaques called "coppers," the raw metal became transformed into objects that were beautiful as well as symbols of wealth and social rank. Coppers could weigh as much as forty pounds and were painted or engraved with crest symbols. Regarded with respect, coppers were an important part of the Northwest Coast potlatch tradition—Native gatherings called by families to commemorate major life events. At potlatches, where feasting, dancing, and gift-giving were lavish, coppers were often given away whole or in pieces as elaborately generous gestures of respect.

To the northeast of Taral, Athabascan Indians living in the vicinity of the White River made utensils and weapons out of copper nuggets they dug from rock deposits with caribou horns. One copper nugget from the area—now in the MacBride Museum in Whitehorse, Yukon Territory—weighed 2,590 pounds.

DAYLIGHT AND DARKNESS

For sixty-seven consecutive days beginning in mid-November and continuing until late January, the sun does not rise in Barrow, Alaska's north-ernmost town. When the sun finally reappears, Barrow's school-children celebrate its arrival with songs. On the flip side, Barrow enjoys eighty-four days of uninterrupted light from mid-May to early August. Winter or summer, the sun never appears to be high in the sky; even the summer sun seems to stretch across the sky rather than climb through it.

Why this low sun and all-or-nothing daylight and darkness? Because the earth is slightly tilted on its axis as it rotates around the sun, sunlight hits the poles at different angles during the year. In summer, when the Northern Hemisphere is nodded toward the sun, daylight hours are long. In the winter, the axis is tipped away from the sun, leaving the North Pole in shadow and darkness.

> For sixty-seven consecutive days in winter, the sun does not rise in Barrow, Alaska.

Even in Alaska the angle can be different from one part of the state to the next, because the place is so big. Ketchikan, in Southeast, averages about 7 hours of light per day in the winter and 17 hours in the summer. Farther north, Fairbanks is about in the middle with approximately 3½ hours of light per day in the winter and more than 20 hours of daylight throughout the summer. Cold-tolerant varieties of flowers and vegetables thrive, and even grow to huge proportions, in the long hours of light; many Alaskans enjoy gardening.

Regardless of the time of year, Alaska has remarkably long twilights. This is because the sun hits northern latitudes at such a low angle. At the equator, where the sun is nearly straight overhead, an early spring twilight is about twenty-four minutes long. In Fairbanks, the same twilight lasts an hour.

Even though the summer sun does go down in northerly parts of the state (except on the summer solstice, day of the midnight sun, around June 21), the brief nights don't get dark—instead they linger in twilight because, for about a month before and a month after the solstice, the sun doesn't sink more than six degrees below the horizon.

See also MIDNIGHT SUN

EARTHQUAKE Alaska has a whole lotta shakin' goin' on: more earthquake activity occurs here than in all the other states put together. In a sense, earthquakes are Alaska's growing pains. Geologically this is a young land, still growing and adjusting.

Between 1974 and 2003, Alaska had 12,053 earthquakes of a magnitude 3.5 or greater. ("Magnitude" has replaced "Richter scale" as the most accurate way to describe the intensity of earthquakes. Generally, a magnitude 1.5 earthquake is about the smallest that can be felt. A tremor of 4.5 causes slight damage, and 8.5 is devastating.)

Ninety percent of Alaska's major earthquakes occur in a narrow band that follows the coast around from Southeast through Southcentral and out the Aleutian Chain. This marks where the Pacific tectonic plate, a giant jigsaw piece of the earth's crust, pushes northwestward parallel to Southeast, and dives under Southcentral, the Alaska Peninsula, and the Aleutian Islands.

Along the line where tectonic plates meet, rocks bend as the plates move. Rocks under the Gulf of Alaska are thought to be capable of bending about ten to sixteen feet before they break and cause an earthquake.

The most destructive earthquake in Alaska's recorded history occurred in the Southcentral part of the state, in the early morning hours of Good Friday, March 27, 1964. Clay soils beneath Anchorage were liquefied by the shaking ground, and many downtown buildings were destroyed. Shock waves were felt as far as seven hundred miles away from the Prince William Sound epicenter. With an assigned magnitude of 9.2, this was the strongest earthquake ever measured in North America and the second strongest in the world—releasing ten million times more energy than the atomic bomb that devastated Hiroshima in World War II.

Miraculously, only 130 people were killed; earthquakes of far less magnitude have taken thousands of lives in other parts of the world. Of the 130 deaths, 119 were tsunami-related, most occurring south of Anchorage in communities exposed to the Gulf of Alaska or Prince William Sound, including Valdez, Whittier, and Kodiak. A small number of tsunami deaths were reported as far away as Oregon and California. The highest wave occurred near Valdez, where an underwater slide triggered a surge that toppled trees 100 feet above tidewater and deposited sand and silt 220 feet above salt water. The town of Valdez had to be moved after the 1964 quake.

For more than two months after Black Friday, Alaskans shuddered with twelve thousand aftershocks of magnitude 3.5 or higher. The extremely violent earthquake permanently rearranged about one hundred thousand square miles of land, deforming earth as much as seventy feet horizontally and thirty feet vertically in places. North of Anchorage, the Matanuska Valley spread five feet wider.

See also WAVE

ERRATIC Like hobos hopping a train out of town, glacial erratics are rocks and boulders that hitched rides on, and in, slow-moving glaciers and were carried along until they were dumped by the melting ice sheets—sometimes hundreds of miles from where they started. Erratics are common around Anchorage, deposited there by one of the five or so glaciers that moved in and out of the Anchorage bowl in the last few million years. The 4,396-foot summit of Mount Susitna, which lies across Cook Inlet from Anchorage, was once buried under a glacier, and is littered with erratics.

These transient boulders are called erratics because they're different from the bedrock beneath them—a granite boulder that appears on top of sedimentary rock, for example. Over time, soils can build around the nomads, so what appears to be a small rock partially buried in the ground can turn into a car-sized surprise—something that seems to happen as soon as someone decides to dig it out. An erratic in Alberta, Canada, reportedly weighed more than 118,000 tons.

FJORD   Fjords are glacially carved valleys that have been invaded by the sea. Usually quite deep, fjords are marked by steep, high sides and a U-shaped profile. In contrast, river-carved valleys tend to be more V-shaped.

The fjords on Alaska's Kenai Peninsula are part of the nearly 650,000-square-mile Kenai Fjords National Park, a place as scenic as the fjords of Norway or New Zealand. Mature coastal forests descend steep mountainsides to the water, as do some glaciers. Cool and wet during the summer, the fjords are home to many

Fjord
(Turnegain Arm, from the estuary end)

marine mammals, including sea otters, whales, sea lions, and seals. Tufted and horned puffins and other seabirds nest here.

Presiding over the Kenai fjords is the immense Harding Icefield, a seven-hundred-square-mile field of ice left over from an ice-age ice cap that once completely covered the Kenai Mountains. Four glaciers over fifteen miles long flow from the ice field today.

See also GLACIER

FOREST Visitors to Alaska's Interior are sometimes surprised that the expanse of wilderness there is not made up of vast forests of big trees—especially if they've come from the rain forests of Southeast.

Alaska has two distinct forest ecosystems: interior and coastal. Forests of the interior ecosystem, which extends from the south slope of the Brooks Range to the Kenai Peninsula and from Canada to Norton Sound, are often referred to as boreal forests. Boreal simply means "of, or relating to, northern regions." Forests of white spruce, paper birch, quaking aspen, black cottonwood, and balsam poplar cover about 32 percent, or about 106 million acres, of the interior ecosystem, with about one-fifth of that classified as commercial forestland. The distribution of forests in Interior Alaska is a patchwork determined largely by fire history, slope, and the presence or absence of permafrost.

In general, climatic conditions in the Interior are too extreme to allow trees to grow very large. Even on the best sites—warm and dry south-facing slopes—a white spruce will rarely grow larger than about two feet in diameter. In contrast, a Sitka spruce in the coastal forest can grow to eight or more feet in diameter.

Most interior forests are stands of two or more tree species; white spruce and birch, for instance, are commonly found together.

The coastal forest ecosystem, where the climate is wet and relatively mild, is where the really big trees are. Alaska's coastal forests are considered temperate rain forests. The coastal forest ecosystem extends from Kodiak Island, around Cook Inlet and down through Southeast.

The dense, coniferous coastal forests are marked by steep

terrain; trees grow up the slopes from sea level to tree line at about two thousand to three thousand feet in elevation. In the southern part of the coastal ecosystem, forests are composed primarily of western hemlock and Sitka spruce, with a scattering of mountain hemlock, western red-cedar, and Alaska cedar. Farther north, the cedars drop out and western hemlock thins out, leaving Sitka spruce as the prime tree. Douglas fir, the characteristic conifer of Pacific Northwest forests, doesn't grow in Alaska.

Alaska's two national forests are the largest and second-largest in the nation. Between them, they comprise an area equal in size to Indiana. The 17-million-acre Tongass National Forest includes more than 70 percent of Southeast, encircling such communities as Petersburg, Sitka, and the state capital, Juneau. The 5.6-million-acre Chugach National Forest surrounds Prince William Sound and includes the Copper River Delta and parts of the Kenai Peninsula. The towns of Seward and Valdez border the Chugach Forest.

> Alaska's two national forests together comprise an area equal in size to Indiana.

The land comprising national forests isn't just forested—in fact, much of it is covered with treeless ice fields and glaciers, wetlands, muskeg, rivers, lakes, rocks, and alpine tundra.

But the forest of trees is what awes the observer. Dense, dark green stands of hemlock and Sitka spruce with a scattering of cedar fill steep slopes like choir members on risers. Red alder lines streams and beaches, and black cottonwood can be found on floodplains. Subalpine and Pacific fir appear occasionally. Filling in the forest gaps and underspaces are blueberries, devil's club, salal, and other shrubs. Moss is everywhere.

More than four hundred species of wildlife live in the two forests. Species that are threatened or endangered elsewhere, such as wolves and grizzly bears, occur here in abundance. More bald eagles can be seen in the Tongass National Forest than anywhere else in the world. Forest streams and rivers provide spawning habitat for more than 25 percent of Alaska's salmon, and millions of shorebirds and waterfowl feed and nest on forest wetlands.

See also ASPEN; BIRCH; CEDAR; HEMLOCK; SPRUCE

FROST HEAVE

FROST HEAVE The infamous frost heaves on some of Alaska's roadways test a car's shocks and a driver's stomach. These roller-coaster humps in the road result when soils freeze and expand, pushing up the road surface or anything else in the way.

Frost heaves occur most noticeably in wet, fine-grained soils of silt or clay—materials that expand as they freeze (the silt and clay themselves don't actually expand as it freezes, but the water that has infiltrated those materials does). Even after soil freezes, groundwater may rise into the frozen ground and freeze, further pushing up the soil. In areas of plentiful groundwater, frost heaves can expand and grow in this way all winter.

Driving too fast over bad heaves can lead to a broken axle or trailer hitch. Pilings are also affected by frost heaves. In fine-grained soils, upward pressure on pilings can easily reach sixty pounds per square inch. Studies have shown that a twenty-inch-diameter piling set four feet deep in soil that freezes at least as deep as the piling can experience pressures of two hundred thousand pounds. The reason pilings don't pop right out of the ground is that in most cases, sideways pressure accounts for about 90 percent of the force. Even so, in some cases frost heaves can lift pilings a foot or more during the winter.

> Frost heaves create roller-coaster humps in roads when soils freeze and expand.

Frost heaving can happen in any frozen ground, but the phenomenon is more noticeable when it lifts a road or a piling.

GLACIER

GLACIER Glaciers are like giant sculpting tools that refashion the face of the earth with their slow-motion modeling. As they move, these bodies of ice carve wide, U-shaped valleys, round off mountaintops, build hummocks and ridges of debris, scour the terrain with the floods they cause, and litter the landscape with erratic rocks and boulders.

Thousands of glaciers cover about 29,000 square miles of Alaska. The largest—twice the size of Rhode Island—is the 2,250-square-mile Bering Glacier complex in the Chugach Mountains of Southcentral Alaska. Thanks to its cool temperatures and tremendous snowfalls, Southcentral holds a quarter to a third of the world's mountain glacier ice; coastal mountains in this region have been under ice for at least the last five million years.

Glaciers form when more snow falls than melts. Over time, snow recrystallizes into ice grains, which are further crystallized by the accumulating weight of new snow falling onto the glacier, into solid, airless ice—in some cases thousands of feet thick and thousands of years old.

Eventually, gravity begins pulling the glacier slowly down-hill—anywhere from an inch to a couple of feet a day. Glaciers move both by sliding and by a conveyor belt–like flow within the ice—like a thick blob of honey oozing down an incline, where the top surface is moving faster than the bottom surface.

Examples of all glacier types are found in Alaska: the familiar alpine glaciers found high on mountain slopes or plateaus; piedmont glaciers, in which two or more glaciers combine to form a fan-shaped mass at the foot of the mountains; tidewater glaciers that extend down to the sea; and valley glaciers, created when alpine glaciers settle into valleys. The ninety-two-mile-long Hubbard Glacier near Yakutat, north of Glacier Bay National Park and Preserve, is the longest valley glacier in North America. Ice fields form when valley glaciers merge, leaving only nunataks (mountain peaks surrounded by ice) and high ridges showing above the snowy surface. The Juneau Icefield covers the mountains of a fifteen-hundred-square-mile area and is the source from which the Mendenhall, Taku, Eagle, and other glaciers flow.

In most cases, sleeping is more interesting than glacier watching, but surging glaciers and calving tidewater glaciers are the exciting exceptions. Surging glaciers can move nearly two hundred feet a day. In the spring of 1986, the Hubbard Glacier surged hundreds of feet in a few weeks, damming Russell Fiord.

Margerie Glacier

Six months later the ice dam broke, releasing 3.5 million cubic feet of water per second into Disenchantment Bay. Geologists believe this might be the largest such event since the Glacial Lake Missoula floods spilled from Montana into the Columbia River valley some fourteen thousand years ago. More recently, the Bering Glacier, southeast of Cordova, began to surge in the spring of 1995, and surged perhaps four miles in about one and a half months. A strip of land only a few miles wide is all that remains between the Bering Glacier and the Gulf of Alaska. If the Bering Glacier does reach the gulf, tanker traffic could be threatened by resulting icebergs.

Icebergs are often born with a spectacular splash and a rumbling roar like thunder as tidewater glaciers calve, or shed, pieces of ice—sometimes as tall as a thirteen-story building—into the sea. Pieces can also calve off the underwater portion of the glacier. These "shooters" surge up unexpectedly in a sudden, turbulent upwelling. Prince William Sound has twenty actively calving tidewater glaciers, the greatest concentration in the state. Le Conte Glacier, located behind Petersburg in Southeast Alaska, is the most southerly active tidewater glacier in North America.

In Southeast Alaska's Glacier Bay, twelve of the bay's eighteen tidewater glaciers are calving. When Captain George Vancouver explored the area in 1794, the shorelines were completely covered with ice and Glacier Bay was a mere indent in the glacier. In the two hundred years or so since then, the glaciers of Glacier Bay have retreated about sixty-five miles—the fastest glacial retreat on that scale known anywhere. The glaciers' speedy retreat and rapid vegetation of the exposed land has made Glacier Bay an internationally renowned outdoor laboratory for the study of plant succession.

See also ERRATIC; FJORD; ICEBERG; MORAINE; NUNATAK

GLORY Glories are round rainbows that circle the shadow of an airplane like a good omen. Also known as Brocken specters or Brocken bows, glories are created when sunlight is refracted, or bent, back in the same direction from which it arrived as it enters water droplets of clouds or mist. In comparison, rainbows are created by a different angle of light refraction through water droplets in the air, and haloes around the sun and moon are created by light refraction through ice crystals in the air.

The size of a glory is directly inverse to the size of the water droplets; the larger the diameter of the glory, the smaller the water droplets. So, look for the largest glories when flying through thin or wispy clouds, where water droplets are probably evaporating and therefore smaller.

Glories can also appear around the shadow of your own head when your back is toward the sun and your shadow falls on mist or fog. Oddly enough, because of the way the light is dispersed, several people observing a glory together will see haloes only around their own head. The phenomenon is common in high-latitude places like Alaska because the sun is so low in the sky. This "side lighting" results in a greater likelihood that a person will come between the sun and some form of mist.

GOLD There's gold in them thar hills—and in them stream-beds, and even on them beaches. Beginning in the mid-1880s, countless small strikes and several major ones have resulted in the extraction of about 33.3 million ounces of gold from Alaska—worth more than $12 billion at today's prices.

Much of Alaska's gold was formed in association with magma, or underground molten rock. Gold is formed when mineral-rich solutions in the molten rock begin to cool. The solutions filter out of the magma and infiltrate adjacent rocks, where continued cooling deposits a sequence of tin, copper, lead, zinc, iron, gold, and mercury. Ores can form when pressure from the superhot magma forces the mineral solution into fractures in nearby rocks, where it cools and crystallizes into veins of minerals known as lodes.

Over time, rain, erosion, and other processes break down the rock that contains the gold. As the rock is broken down, the gold may be released and washed into placer deposits. A placer is a gold-bearing layer of sand or gravel formed when gold weathered out of its parent rock is washed into a streambed or onto a beach, where it settles.

Placer mining usually involves digging up placer deposits and running the debris through sluice boxes, where water is used to wash away the gravel and sand, while trapping the heavier gold that settles at the bottom.

Gold dredges are building-sized digging and washing contraptions used in larger placer mining operations. Dredging tore up the landscape; mine tailings—long hummock-sized lumps that are a by-product of dredging—are noticeable around Fairbanks and other Alaskan gold mining areas.

The other common type of gold mining is called hard rock mining, and involves extracting gold-bearing quartz veins from larger rock formations, then crushing the quartz to get the gold.

Pure gold is twenty-four karats, although much of the gold used to make jewelry is gold-copper alloy; the greater the copper content, the fewer the karats.

Gold was first discovered in Alaska in 1848 in the Russian River on the Kenai Peninsula. Other significant discoveries include the 1880 Gold Creek strike at Juneau, the 1898 discovery of gold near Nome, and Felix Pedro's 1902 discovery of gold in the Fairbanks area. In Alaska's mining history, about 25 percent of the gold has been extracted from the hills of the Tanana Valley in the Fairbanks area, 20 percent from mines in the Juneau area, 15 percent from the area around Nome, and the rest from scattered sites around the state. Nome's fantastically rich deposits were found in the sands of the beach along the Bering Sea. Miners working the beach could make twenty to a hundred dollars a day with just a shovel and pan. The Nome goldfields yielded the biggest nugget found in the state, which weighed nearly seven pounds and measured seven by four by two inches.

> **Gold forms when mineral-rich solutions in molten rock begin to cool. Ores form under pressure.**

Gold mining was a mainstay of the Alaska economy until World War II. Today, Alaskans still pan for fun and mine gold commercially.

HOARFROST AND RIME In Alaska, Jack Frost delivers two kinds of ice crystal glaze: hoarfrost and rime.

Hoarfrost forms when air becomes too frigid to hold its water vapor. When water vapor condenses out of the air to settle on a cold surface, it changes directly from vapor to ice crystal. (If the vapor lands on a warm surface, it becomes liquid.) The shape hoarfrost takes—from delicate crystalline patterns on windows to the feathery forms that encrust trees and men's beards—depends mostly on temperatures, the amount of water vapor present, and the nature of the surface upon which the vapor falls.

Rime is created when supercooled clouds or fog sweep over an area, depositing complex, often crusted crystal structures on cold objects in the path of the mist. Trees near hot springs or warm rivers are often coated with this type of frost. When a breeze is present, rime accumulates, building granular ice tufts that project into the wind as droplets freeze on contact.

HOT SPRING This is one kind of hot water Alaskans like to find themselves in. Natural hot springs are scattered across Alaska from southern Southeast to the Brooks Range.

Hot springs form when water finds its way deep into the earth via fractures or faults, becomes heated by subsurface temperatures, then travels back to the surface through other faults and fractures. Water in the pool at Chena Hot Springs, sixty-two miles northeast of Fairbanks, is heated about two miles below the surface before it emerges to soak bathers' weary bones.

Water doesn't have to come into contact with molten rock in order to be heated; on average, earth's temperature increases about 75°F per mile of depth, so solid rock can be hot enough to significantly raise water temperatures. Many of Alaska's hot springs occur near "intrusive granitic plutons," formations created long ago when molten rock pushed, or intruded, into neighboring rock, then solidified. These plutons, made of relatively insoluble granitic rock, can have deep fractures that tend to remain open and clear, so water can circulate freely down into the earth, become heated, and flow back out.

Although rock doesn't *have* to be molten to create hot springs, volcanic activity certainly does create thermal features at the surface. In the volcanically active Aleutian Islands, subsurface temperatures increase more rapidly, producing boiling springs and superheated fumaroles in addition to hot springs.

Of Alaska's 124 identified geothermal areas, only about seventeen have been developed in any way for public bathing—

White Sulphur
Hot Spring

and only a few of those are accessible by road. Alaskans trek to their favorite hot waters, developed or not, via boat, plane, or snow machine, on foot, or even by dogsled. A handful of Alaska's hot springs provide resort-type facilities, including Chena Hot Springs; Circle Hot Springs, 136 miles northeast of Fairbanks; Manley Hot Springs,

160 miles west of Fairbanks; and Bell Hot Springs, 40 air miles northeast of Ketchikan.

Native Alaskans were the first to appreciate the Great Land's hot springs. Aleuts soaked in thermal springs at Adak, Atka, Akutan, and other islands in the Aleutian Chain. The village site near Port Moller Hot Springs on the north side of the Alaska Peninsula has been occupied intermittently for the past three thousand years. Miners and trappers were quick to latch onto the pleasures of northern hot springs, changing such Native appellations as Kruzagampah and Hoonah to names like Pilgrim and Tenakee.

ICEBERG These floating ice islands can be a navigational hazard to boaters, but are floating resorts for seals and birds, who rest comfortably on them, safe from most predators. Icebergs are chunks of ice that have been shed or "calved" off glaciers that extend all the way down to the sea or a lake. Of varying size, icebergs can be as small as a Volkswagen or as big as a castle. Alaska's record iceberg, calved into Icy Bay in May 1977, measured 346 feet long and 297 feet wide, and rose 99 feet above the waterline. Drifting with the currents, icebergs lend an air of mystery and adventure to Alaska's waters.

Nearly everyone is familiar with the "tip of the iceberg" concept, and it's true. As a general rule, 75 percent to 80 percent of an iceberg's mass is underwater. This doesn't necessarily mean icebergs are stable, however: they frequently roll over or split apart with no warning as they slowly melt. How high a berg floats is affected by its size, its density, and how much sediment it holds. Icebergs carrying an especially large amount of debris may hang slightly below the surface or even sink to the bottom. Because the salt water surrounding the terminus of a tidewater glacier may actually be a few degrees below the freezing point of freshwater, a freshwater iceberg sunk near the glacier's edge may remain unmelted indefinitely.

Color provides clues to an iceberg's story. Blue bergs have no air bubbles, an indication that the ice has been thoroughly compressed and is probably from a section of the glacier that is quite old. Greenish black icebergs have likely calved off the glacier's

Alaska's record iceberg measured 346 feet long and 297 feet wide, and rose 99 feet above the waterline.

bottom, and darkly striped or dirty-looking bergs contain rubble, possibly from where two tributary glaciers merged.

Glacier Bay is an excellent place to see icebergs; eighteen glaciers there extend all the way down to the water and regularly calve icebergs into the bay. Mendenhall Glacier near Juneau calves icebergs into Mendenhall Lake, and Portage Lake near Anchorage may contain icebergs calved off Portage Glacier.

See also GLACIER

JADE Jade takes the green of the Gulf of Alaska and wraps it in stone. This is Alaska's state gem, and no wonder.

Most Alaskan jade is found above the Arctic Circle in the vicinity of the Kobuk and Shungnak Rivers north of the Seward Peninsula. On display at the University of Alaska Fairbanks Museum is a 3,550-pound jade boulder, as big as a coffee table, from the Kobuk River area. The top has been polished flat and satiny as a calm sea.

Jade is the finest, gem-quality form of the mineral jadeite. (Gemstones are minerals that are prized for their beauty; a gemstone becomes a gem when it is cut, shaped, and polished.)

Alaska's jade can range in color from Gulf of Alaska green to brown, black, yellow, white—even red. Most valued are stones with black, white, and green marbling. About a quarter of the jade mined in Alaska is of gem quality and is used for jewelry. Alaskan artists find jade to be an elegant medium for sculpture; jade is also crafted into clock faces, bookends, chess sets, and other items.

The word jade comes from the Spanish *piedra de ijada*, which means "stone of the side"—a reference to the belief that if pressed against one's side, jade could cure kidney disorders.

MIDNIGHT SUN The poet Robert Service was right:

"There are strange things done in the midnight sun. . . ." With all that light, regular schedules are nearly impossible. After a winter of darkness, just try to get people inside when they can play night baseball with no lights, then come home and weed their garden after the game. In many families suppertime edges toward 9 P.M. and kids are out riding their bikes at 10. And anyway, it's hard to sleep in daylight, even if it is 11 P.M. Sleeping is for winter, when there's no shortage of darkness.

Alaska's night light is especially celebrated on the longest day of the summer, the summer solstice, which occurs on June 21 or 22. At and above the Arctic Circle (66°32 N), the sun doesn't dip below the horizon at all on that one day. Even the day before and the day after solstice, the sunset is so shallow that light refraction (the bending of light rays) makes the sun visible above the horizon. In some places just below the Arctic Circle it's possible to see the midnight sun by climbing to a high point, like Eagle Summit north of Fairbanks.

See also ARCTIC CIRCLE; DAYLIGHT AND DARKNESS

MORAINE Much of the topography of Southeast and Southcentral Alaska was shaped by glacial action; U-shaped valleys and fjords are two of the more obvious landscape forms created by glaciers. Moraines—jumbles, piles, and ridges of rocks and boulders deposited by glaciers—are more subtle to discern, as they are usually covered with layers of soil and vegetation and tend to blend into the landscape. A moraine at the foot of a glacier may create a dam that causes a lake to form as the glacier melts; evidence of other types of moraines include ridges in, or at the edges of, glacially carved valleys.

Terminal moraines form at the foot, or terminus—or "snout"—of a glacier. As a glacier creeps downhill, rocks and debris stuck in the bottom of the glacier scour and grind away at the mountainside like coarse sandpaper. The glacier continues to collect more rocks as it moves, sometimes picking up rocks on its upper surface when the mountainside above sheds rocks through rock slides and the cleaving effect that occurs when water in the rock freezes and thaws.

Slowly, material imbedded in the glacier is transported to the terminus, where the melting glacier drops its load of glacial till— a conglomerate of rocky debris that includes everything from silt and sand to gravel and boulders. (You can tell glacially deposited till from stream-deposited rock because glaciers don't sort their freight. If, for instance, in a road cut you see many different-sized rocks imbedded in what looks like clay or silt, you could be look-ing at a moraine. But if the rocks are mostly the same size, they have likely been sorted and deposited by the running water of a river, stream, or flood.) Terminal moraines can really build up when the glacier's terminus melts at about the same speed as the glacier creeps.

Lateral moraines are ridges of jumbled rock that have accumulated along the sides of a glacier. When two glaciers merge on the way down a mountain, their lateral moraines (if they have them) can combine to form what geologists call a medial moraine. When the glacier eventually melts away, the medial moraine appears as an irregular ridge in the middle of a glacial valley.

See also ERRATIC; GLACIER

MOUNTAIN From the highest peaks of the Alaska Range to the modest mountains of the Igichuk Hills, Alaska has thirty-nine distinct mountain ranges.

Alaska's larger mountain ranges are like room dividers, sepa-rating the state into areas with distinctly different characteristics. Weather and habitat can be drastically dissimilar on different sides of a range.

The Brooks Range—an extensive east-west mountain range reaching across the state north of the Arctic Circle—separates arctic Alaska from the Interior. Mountains of the Brooks Range inhibit the movement of cold air blowing off the Arctic Ocean. Part of the 19.6-million-acre Arctic National Wildlife Refuge lies in the eastern Brooks Range.

Far to the south of the Brooks Range, the Alaska Range follows the general contour of Alaska's south coast, although its arc of mountains is one hundred to two hundred miles inland.

Mount McKinley
(Denali)

The six-hundred-mile-long range reaches from about Southwest Alaska to the Canadian border and is considered the southern limit of the Interior region. Mountains of the Alaska Range help to limit and dry out wet air flowing from the south coastal area of the state. The 20,320-foot Denali (Mount McKinley)—the tallest mountain in North America—is the shining star of the Alaska Range.

The Alaska Range formed about ten million to twenty million years ago from uplifting forces associated with the Denali Fault, which passes near the headquarters of Denali National Park and Preserve. Denali's spectacular height may have something to do with being at a bend in the fault. The Denali Fault traces an arc from Southeast Alaska, through the Alaska Range, and west to Bristol Bay. The Alaska Highway follows the fault from the Canadian border to Northway.

Named McKinley in 1896 for a presidential candidate from Ohio, the mountain's original Athabascan name, Denali, means "the high one." In 1975 the state of Alaska officially renamed the mountain Denali, which the state Geographic Names Board claims is the proper name for the mountain. However, the federal Board of Geographic Names has taken no action, and congressional legislation has been introduced to retain the McKinley name in perpetuity. The mountain is in Denali National Park and Preserve, formerly McKinley National Park, located about 121 miles south of Fairbanks and 237 miles north of Anchorage.

The parkland surrounding Denali is rich in wildlife, with about 155 species of birds and 37 species of mammals, including grizzly bears, moose, caribou, wolverines, Dall sheep, and wolves. Supporting the birds and mammals are a variety of habitat types, including wet and dry tundra, taiga, white and black spruce forests, and woodlands of aspen, birch, and poplar.

South of the Alaska Range, in the southeast corner of the main part of the state, is a national park encompassing the Wrangell–St. Elias and Chugach mountain ranges. The largest unit of land in the national park system, Wrangell–St. Elias National Park and Preserve contains the greatest number of peaks over 14,500 feet in North America, and nine of the sixteen highest peaks in the United States. At 18,008 feet, Mount St. Elias is the second-tallest peak in the nation. Not surprisingly, the area also holds the greatest concentration of glaciers on the continent. The Denali Fault forms the northern boundary of the St. Elias mountain block. The park also contains many significant prehistoric and historic sites, including ancient Native villages and camps.

> **Nine of the sixteen highest peaks in the United States are in Alaska's Wrangell–St. Elias Range.**

MUSKEG Muskegs are basically very old wetlands. Composed of plants in various stages of slow decay, peat bogs, as they're also known, are common all over Alaska and form most readily in cool, wet areas where soils are poorly drained.

Under most conditions, when plants die, bacteria and fungi work with oxygen to break down the vegetative matter in relatively short order. But in the water-saturated, low-oxygen, acidic muskeg environment, bacteria and fungi can't accomplish their decomposing mission as effectively. As a result, incompletely decomposed debris from dead plants accumulates, forming peat—the same fibrous material you can buy in bales. When a wetland has amassed one foot of peat, it is reclassified as a muskeg. It may take a thousand years to build up one foot of peat, and layers in some Alaska muskegs are twenty feet thick.

Sphagnum moss (*Sphagnum* spp.), which holds fifteen to

thirty times its own weight in water, is muskeg's dominant plant form, but specialized wildflowers and shrubs also grow here, including marsh violet, round-leafed sundew, swamp gentian, and bog cranberries and blueberries.

Few tree species can grow in muskeg, but black spruce *(Picea mariana)* and shore pine *(Pinus contorta)* manage to take root in the inhospitable landscape—even though they may grow only five to fifteen feet in three hundred years.

Muskeg, which is essentially a surface mat floating on a very soggy bog, can be treacherous to traverse—like trying to walk on wet, shredded foam floating on a pool. Some muskegs are quite deep, and offer no toeholds to climb out. Animals including wolves, brown and black bears, and weasels forage around the edges of muskeg, often hunting the shrews and voles that may be active all year in Alaska's more southerly bogs.

Blue grouse bring their young to muskegs to feed on cranberries, bog blueberries, and insects, and the shorebird yellowlegs prefers the mossy ground of muskeg for nesting.

See also WETLAND

NIGHT AIRGLOW
Night airglow—a dim, atmospheric luminescence—is the reason why stars don't seem as brilliant in the Alaska sky as in the Lower 48. Night airglow can outshine stars so much so that the weakest points of light fade completely from sight, and even the brightest stars lose some twinkle power.

A relative of northern lights, night airglow is produced when solar radiation charges certain gas particles, particularly oxygen, forty miles above the earth. This sky night-light has a real effect on perceived darkness, even though the illumination is so subtle that only informed observers would notice. Brightest at northern latitudes, night airglow can produce more nighttime light for Alaska than all the stars together.

Combined airglow and starlight provide enough light to see relatively well at night, especially if there is snow on the ground for reflection. Add the aurora and a moon, and you can just about read a book.

See also NORTHERN LIGHTS

NOCTILUCENT CLOUD
Northern lights aren't the only evanescent beauties in Alaskan skies. Central Alaska in mid- to late summer is one of the better places in the Northern Hemisphere to see rare noctilucent clouds, described in a science article (in not-so-scientific language) as "blue-white spiderwebs laced across the twilight sky . . . wispy filigree in the heavens." This unusual atmospheric phenomenon is seen only north of the forty-fifth latitude (Montana's southern border runs along latitude forty-five).

While most clouds and weather occur in the first six to twelve vertical miles of sky (the troposphere), noctilucent clouds form fifty miles up in the mesosphere—above the level in the atmosphere where meteors typically burn out.

These clouds are most visible immediately after sunset (or before sunrise) when the sky is a deep shade of blue and the brightest stars are beginning to appear. Light coming from the sun as it hangs just below the horizon illuminates the uncommon clouds against the darkened sky. Noctilucent clouds may be visible during the day, but are indistinguishable from high cirrus clouds to the observer on the ground. Only when the low-angled sun is shining on the upper mesosphere can we feel confident that visible wispy clouds are noctilucent clouds.

The exact physical makeup of noctilucent clouds remains a mystery, since very little water vapor—the common ingredient of most clouds—is found that high. Scientists speculate that noctilucent clouds consist of ice-coated particles of meteoric dust.

NORTHERN LIGHTS (Aurora Borealis)
An arc of pale green light reaches across the dark sky; soon the arc begins to shimmer and undulate with drape-like folding. Perhaps in a few hours the arc will intensify into a broad, waving banner dancing with pinks and blues.

Through time, people have explained this strange celestial show called the northern lights in different ways. Some Alaska Native peoples believed the lights were torches carried by old souls leading the newly dead to the afterworld; others said the lights were caused by spirits playing football with a walrus head. Much later in Alaska's history, treasure-seeking newcomers declared that the aurora was light reflecting off the Mother Lode of gold. Some claimed—and even still claim—that the lights make a crackling or swishing noise. And then there's the theory that northern lights come closer if you whistle to them. . . .

Scientists haven't yet detected auroral sound—nor does the aurora come when it's called. But we do know this: northern lights are caused by an electrical discharge resulting from the interaction between solar wind and the earth's magnetic field.

Solar wind is a stream of particles that blows from the sun toward earth. The wind is caused by solar flares, explosions of gases on the sun's surface that erupt with enough force to splinter the gas atoms apart into electrons and protons.

Fortunately, earth is surrounded by a magnetic shield that causes these particles of solar wind to stream around our planet instead of bombarding it. As the solar wind brushes against the magnetic shield, electrons within earth's atmosphere are charged; charged electrons strike gas particles in the upper atmosphere and create an electrical discharge that we see as light.

Color of the northern lights is determined by the type of gas being struck and by the energy of the particle striking it. The most common color, greenish yellow, comes from interactions with oxygen about 60 miles high. Oxygen at 150 miles up produces rare all-red auroras. Ionized nitrogen molecules are responsible for blue light, and purplish red edges are created by neutral nitrogen molecules.

> Some people believe the northern lights make a crackling or swishing noise.

The strength and frequency of northern lights are tied to the strength and frequency of solar flares.

Why is the aurora usually seen only at high latitudes? Because the magnetic field around the earth is shaped like an apple, dipping in at either end (the poles) to connect with a core. The magnetic field controls the location of the aurora by guiding electrical currents down toward the poles. In

1967, scientists verified that auroras at the north and south poles are often identical, appearing simultaneously in the same form—a condition known as conjugacy. (The southern aurora is called the aurora australis.)

The aurora produces more than just a visual phenomenon. The electrical field associated with the aurora creates a current in the top layer of the atmosphere. That current induces a parallel current that flows through the ground and can cause corrosion in pipes; corrosion in the trans-Alaska pipeline has been attributed in part to the aurora borealis. Radio communication systems and power transmission lines are also occasionally disrupted by auroral activity.

Alaska and eastern Siberia have the brightest auroras in the world. Tourists from all over the world come to Alaska to view them. Northern lights appear over Fairbanks more than two hundred nights per year, usually beginning in September and continuing through early spring. (The aurora occurs in summer too, but is outshone by the midnight sun.) Optimal viewing seasons are spring and fall; best viewing time is about 10 P.M. to 2 A.M. But each night is different. Lights may develop fully and last for hours, or stay a faint, fleeting glimmer. Northern lights can also be observed from aircraft. For the best chance of a view, sit on the left side of the plane if you're southbound, and on the right if you're headed north.

See also NIGHT AIRGLOW

NUNATAK In parts of some Alaskan mountain ranges, vast sheets of ice cover all but the tallest, solitary peaks. Northern peoples called these solemn, dark heads *nunataks*—"lonely peaks."

By definition, a nunatak is an isolated knob or peak of bedrock that projects above an ice field's or glacier's surface and is completely surrounded by ice. During times of extensive glaciation (ice ages), nunataks were rare islands of terra firma in a sea of packed snow.

Even when all the ice is long gone, former nunataks are easily recognized as prominent, sharp peaks rising above terrain that has been rounded by glacial force. It's hard to imagine an ice sheet thick enough to tuck up around a nunatak's throat, but twenty thousand years ago, some Alaskan ice sheets were nearly a mile thick.

In Alaska, nunataks are still visible rising above some glaciers and ice fields, including the Hubbard Glacier near Yakutat and the Juneau Icefield above Juneau.

Biologists surmise that certain geographically separated but genetically linked plant and animal populations found today survived the periodic ice ages on neighboring nunataks.

See also GLACIER

OIL The Prudhoe Bay oil field on the North Slope at the very top of Alaska holds an estimated 12 billion or more barrels of oil—more than can be found in any other oil field in North America. This dark, rich crude is pumped out of shale deposited more than two million years ago in the early Jurassic period, when the world was warm and dinosaurs roamed the Northland.

Scientists don't know exactly how oil is formed, but most believe that today's oil and gas were yesterday's marine microorganisms. As the tiny creatures died, their bodies collected on the seafloor, where they were covered with sediment. Eventually the sediment hardened into rock; over time, many layers of sediment could have been deposited. Heat and pressure from the

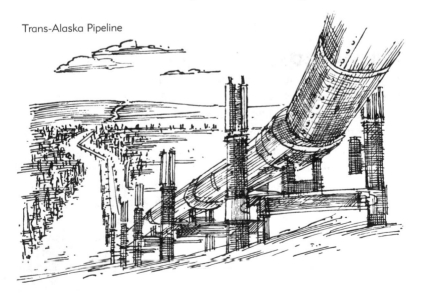

Trans-Alaska Pipeline

covering rock layers are thought to have combined with bacterial processes to transform the sea creatures into petroleum; higher heat caused lighter natural gas to form from the heavier oil.

As early as 1921, oil companies were surveying land north of the Brooks Range for possible drilling sites. In 1957, Atlantic Richfield discovered oil on the Kenai Peninsula, after which Union Oil found a large gas field at Kalifonsky Beach, also on the Kenai Peninsula. Amoco found the first offshore oil in Cook Inlet in 1962. The Prudhoe Bay oil field was discovered in 1968 by Atlantic Richfield Company and Exxon. In 1984, Shell Western discovered oil at Seal Island, twelve miles northwest of Prudhoe Bay. Since 1957, the oil and gas industry has invested over $45 billion in Alaska exploration, oil-field development, and construction of the trans-Alaska oil pipeline.

The eight-hundred-mile-long oil pipeline crosses three mountain ranges, more than eight hundred rivers and streams, and three major earthquake faults. In the spring of 1988, it was estimated that half of Prudhoe Bay's recoverable oil had been extracted. Oil and natural gas are also being pumped out of Cook Inlet from eighteen floating oil platforms. In all, Alaska provides the nation with about a quarter of its domestic production. A little over half of the oil used in the United States is imported, making Alaska's contribution to national consumption about one-eighth. Since 1987, Alaska and Texas have alternated as the number-one oil-producing state.

PERMAFROST The cook who invented baked Alaska—cake covered with ice cream, topped with meringue—must have been inspired by permafrost. In Alaska's permafrost-affected ground, permafrost is like the ice cream layer, the substrate is the cake, and a temperate topping of muskeg, tundra, or topsoil is the meringue.

Sub-ground that remains frozen for two or more years is classified as permafrost. The entire Arctic region is covered by continuous, or uninterrupted, permafrost, sometimes beginning only a foot or so below the surface and reaching down as far as two thousand feet. Discontinuous, or patchy, permafrost is widespread throughout the Interior and is also found in Southcentral.

Because frozen ground can't easily absorb and wick away water, areas of permafrost are often overlain with boggy habitats and small lakes. This inability of the soil to absorb water also means that rivers in permafrost areas can receive 30 to 40 percent more runoff than rivers of comparable size outside the frozen zone. As a consequence, arctic and subarctic rivers often carry heavy silt loads and are prone to flooding.

Trees grow only reluctantly on permafrost, so treeless boggy areas or expanses of severely stunted black spruce indicate the possible presence of permafrost.

> The entire Arctic region is covered by permafrost, sometimes reaching down two thousand feet.

Structures built on permafrost sites can collapse, or at least seriously settle, if the ground melts as a result of the construction activity. Flooding can also occur when the ground melts. Over half of the trans-Alaska oil pipeline was built aboveground to keep hot oil away from cold soil. The pipeline support pilings in permafrost areas contain a special cooling fluid that naturally circulates through the piling, constantly dissipating heat through radiator fins visible at the top.

See also TAIGA; TUNDRA

PINGO Ice is at the heart of many of Alaska's unique land formations, as it is in pingos—soil-covered mounds of ice from about 50 feet to 1,300 feet across and 5 feet to 160 feet tall. The Inuit called them *pinguq*, "conical hills."

The pingo's ice core is fed by underground water. In a warmer climate, the water would simply flow up as a spring, but in the colder parts of Alaska, in areas underlain by permafrost, water may freeze underground before it reaches the surface. As more groundwater wells up and is also frozen, the earth above it is pushed up, forming a hillock.

Pinguq provide high ground on the flat arctic plain, where they often form on old lake sites as silt gradually freezes and expands. In the Interior, pingos tend to be smaller and may be covered with stands of birch or aspen, in contrast with the surrounding willows, mosses, and scrub spruce.

See also PERMAFROST

RIVER   In such a wild, roadless place as Alaska, rivers are important travel corridors for both people and animals. Indeed, with 365,000 miles of waterway, Alaska has far more river than road.

Alaska's three thousand rivers are divided among about twelve major river systems: the Colville, Noatak, and Kobuk systems of Northern Alaska; the Yukon and its tributaries, the Koyukuk and Tanana Rivers, of Interior Alaska; the Kuskokwim, Susitna, and Copper Rivers of Southwestern and Southcentral; and the Tatshenshini–Alsek, Taku, and Stikine Rivers of Southeast. The nature of Alaska's rivers and streams is as diverse as Alaska's wildlife and people, and runs the gamut from small, clear streams burbling through old-growth forests to massive, wide, and sometimes braided glacier rivers that seem to cut through broad valleys with an agenda.

Yukon River

Glacial rivers, such as the Knik River near Anchorage and the Nenana River of the Interior, appear milky from their heavy loads of silt, or "glacial flour," released into the river from melting glaciers. Fish live in the cloudy rivers, but usually move into clearer water to spawn. A Nenana River riverboat captain likes to say that glacial rivers are too dry to drink and too wet to plow. On warm days in the Interior, melting glaciers can cause river levels to rise dramatically.

The Yukon River (which is not a glacial river) is the longest river in Alaska and king of the river road. Archaeological evidence indicates that people may have been living along the Yukon perhaps more than twenty thousand years ago. The Yukon watershed drains a third of Alaska, 330,000 square miles—all the water from all the tributaries and all the runoff from all the rain and snow in this huge expanse of land drains into the Yukon River, which carries its watery load out to the Bering Sea, where it dumps 1.9 million gallons every second.

From its headwaters in British Columbia, the Yukon flows northwest into Alaska, then bends southwest at Fort Yukon on the Arctic Circle, traveling 2,000 miles in all; 1,400 of those miles in Alaska, across broad floodplains flanked by high bluffs and forested hills, through narrow valleys between mountains, past birch hills, and across tundra flats. The Yukon is the fifth-largest river in North America and the third-largest in the United States behind the Missouri and Mississippi. Unlike those Outside rivers, the muscular Yukon has never been dammed. Only one bridge crosses the river in the whole state (of course, out of the Yukon's 1,400 Alaska miles, only three roads connected to a road system even approach the river). The bridge, part of the Dalton Highway to Prudhoe Bay, is near Stevens Village just south of the Arctic Circle.

Historically, two Native groups occupied the Yukon valley: the Yupik people, who lived along the Bering Sea Coast to about 250 miles upriver, and the Athabascan people, who occupied the land upriver into Canada. Most villages were established on the north bank of the river, because that is the bank apparently preferred by migrating king, coho, and chum salmon—millions of which still return to the Yukon river system to spawn. Life along the Yukon was, and continues to be, centered around salmon. Some Native Alaskans still operate fish wheels (devices powered by the river current to scoop fish from the water) on the Yukon. A trip down the river today can be a trip back through time; during salmon runs, seasonal fish camps of Native Alaskans dot the banks, marked by tents, dogs, children, and racks of drying salmon. Many of the people in the forty or so small, rural communities along the Yukon still rely on salmon for food.

See also HUMAN SETTLEMENT; SALMON

SAD   Many Alaskans say it's not the cold that gets to them in winter, it's the darkness. In a sense, depression can be considered a natural feature—or at least an occasional by-product—of the Alaskan environment. Thought to be caused by reduced daylight, we used to call it the blues, but researchers have given northern depression a name: seasonal affective disorder, or SAD. Some professionals believe as many as 25 percent of people living at higher latitudes are affected.

In contrast to someone who suffers from cabin fever, in which a person becomes restless and anxious to get out and do something after being confined indoors, people with SAD feel tired, cranky, and apathetic. They don't *want* to go out.

> Seasonal affective disorder, or SAD, affects as many as 25 percent of people living at higher latitudes.

One physiological theory for SAD points to the hormone melatonin, after discoveries that melatonin levels in the blood increase dramatically as the days grow shorter. One remedy for SAD sufferers is to sit under artificial lights that produce wavelengths similar to natural light. This seems to reduce the amount of melatonin the body produces, resulting in a concurrent improvement in attitude and emotional state.

Another explanation for SAD is that the long periods of darkness trigger changes in a person's internal clock. Severely depressed people are often out of sync with their circadian rhythms—the twenty-four-hour cycles by which we

arrange our lives. When sleeping and eating patterns are disrupted, depression may result. Keeping to a regular schedule
seems to help.

See also THE BUSH; DAYLIGHT AND DARKNESS

SASTRUGI Sastrugi are cold and wind incarnate. The dune-
like ridges of hard-crusted snow are most common in polar
regions, but can form wherever the air is frigid and strong winds
blow snow over a relatively flat surface—elements that may come
together in any number of places throughout the Interior and
northern regions of Alaska.

Carved so cleanly and sharply by the wind, sastrugi look like
sculpted, permanent landforms. In fact, they are more like sand
dunes, and are constantly being reshaped by the wind. But unlike
sand dunes, sastrugi's ridges are often aligned parallel to the wind.

SEA ICE The center of the Arctic Ocean, where the sea caps the
globe, is covered with a permanent sheet of ice ten to fifteen feet
thick and more—the polar ice pack. Every year, beginning in mid-
September, additional sheets of "annual ice" grow from the edge of
the polar ice pack toward the coast of Alaska (seawater freezes at
around 28.8°F—about three degrees below the freezing point for
freshwater). At the same time, ice begins to grow out from the
shorelines of Alaska's northerly coasts; this shore ice is called "fast
ice." Between the ice spreading out from the polar basin and ice
spreading up from Alaska's shore, the Arctic Ocean between Alaska
and the North Pole is essentially ice-covered during the winter.
Although it's frozen, the ice pack is still very dynamic.

Jostled by winds and currents, the annual pack ice becomes
broken and jumbled, forming a puzzle of interlocking floes
six to ten feet thick that are in constant motion. The surface
of the ice isn't necessarily smooth: winds sometimes push drifting
ice floes up against each other or against shore ice, forming
huge ice walls.

When ice floes separate, or when an ice sheet cracks, channels of water called leads are exposed. Like other habitat "edges"

(the edge of a forest, edge of a stream, a beach), leads are likely places of animal activity; marine mammals tend to congregate at leads because of enhanced food supply. Winds over a lead may cause upwelling of sea currents, raising food organisms toward the surface, and sunlight on the water encourages plankton growth. A concentration of plankton may draw plankton-eating fish, which may attract fish-eating mammals, which may draw mammal-eating mammals. Leads are also convenient passages in and out of the water for seals, which haul out onto the ice to rest—and for the polar bears that hunt the seals.

People, polar bears, and arctic foxes travel over the relatively stable fast ice and onto drifting ice to journey out where the fishing and hunting may be better. Polar bears, seals, and walruses ride drifting floes in search of food and safety. In spring, the fast ice melts or floats away, leaving the Arctic Coast ice-free during the brief summer.

In early 2011, scientists observed record lows in "the giant jigsaw puzzle" of sea ice on the Arctic Ocean. A shrinking ice pack would threaten the well-being of a wide range of wildlife species and human communities in Alaska.

See also ARCTIC FOX; ARCTIC OCEAN; DAYLIGHT AND DARKNESS; POLAR BEAR

SNOW Snow is winter's silver lining, making amends for the cold with offerings of protection, recreation, and beauty.

"Blanket of snow" has a literal meaning to plants and small, nonhibernating ground birds and animals: temperatures under seven inches of new snow can be as much as 50°F warmer than surface temperatures.

To Alaska's restless humans, snow offers something to traverse via skis, dogsled, snowshoes, or snow machine, although anything with runners comes to a rasping halt at about –50°F. At such temperatures, ice crystals don't melt with friction into a gliding surface; they just roll around somewhat like sand.

Just as artists need many words to describe the color blue, northern Native peoples like to have just the right terms for snow's multiple personalities. *Upsik* is snow hardened by wind, from which some northern peoples carve blocks to build igloos. *Annui,* falling snow, becomes *qali* when it sticks to tree branches, and *det-thlok* when it piles up on the ground deep enough that walking requires snowshoes. *Siqoq* is snow blowing at ground level. It is said that Native dialects contain some two hundred words to fully describe what the English language can only euphemistically call "the white stuff"—or, as Alaskan workers call it when the first snowfall portends the end of the construction season, "termination dust."

> Temperatures under seven inches of snow can be as much as 50°F warmer than surface temperatures.

Snow crystals form when water vapor freezes around a nucleus of dust, dirt, ash, broken snow crystal, or other environmental particulate high in the atmosphere. Laws of probability, not laws of physics, dictate that no two snow crystals will be alike. So many variables go into the creation of a crystal (temperature, humidity, wind, type of nucleus, number of water vapor molecules) that duplication seems unlikely—although seven basic crystal categories have been identified, including stellar (star), plate, column, and needle. Depending on conditions, a thousand or more crystals may aggregate into a single snowflake.

Not all of Alaska is inundated with great dumps of snow. At Alaska's northernmost town, Barrow, only about two feet of snow fall in a winter. Because of its cold, dry air, Barrow has one of the lowest rates of precipitation in the state. At the other end of the state, Valdez, on Prince William Sound, more than makes up for Barrow, with an annual snowfall of nearly twenty-seven feet. Thompson Pass, on the Richardson Highway between Glennallen and Valdez, is one of Alaska's snowiest spots. In the winter of 1952–53, more than eighty feet of snow fell—almost twenty-five feet in February alone. In December 1955, five feet of snow fell there in twenty-four hours.

SUN DOG Because of ice crystals in the air, Alaska's sky is a terrific stage for optical phenomena. Sun dogs are favorite stage hands: two spots of light flanking the sun, occasionally showing tails of white light.

When sunlight is refracted (bent) through ice crystals in the air, a pale red-and-blue halo may appear around the sun. The sun dogs, or mock suns, are on the halo, aligned horizontally on either side of the sun.

Refraction of light through ice crystals produces a whole range of colorful sky shiners—including arcs, spots, and patches. Light reflecting, rather than refracting, off ice crystals creates whitish phenomena such as the vertical shafts of light known as sun pillars.

Light refraction through water droplets, as opposed to ice crystals, creates other sky phenomena including rainbows and circular bows called glories. Northern lights are not caused by ice crystals or water droplets.

See also GLORY; NORTHERN LIGHTS

TAIGA   The sparse forests of stunted trees fringing earth's northern tree limit are called taiga, Russian for "land of little sticks." Just as mountains have a line above which trees don't grow, so does the earth. On a mountain, forests give way to treeless alpine habitat; on the planet, trees give way to tundra in arctic and subarctic regions.

Taiga woodlands seem scraggly compared with the rain forests of Southeast Alaska, but things that grow there perhaps deserve even more respect for surviving such harsh circumstances. A four-hundred-year-old taiga spruce may be only fifty feet tall. Along with white and black spruce, other taiga trees and plants include aspen, birch, tamarack, willows, blueberries, wild roses, mosses, and lichens.

Most correctly, the term taiga is used for the boreal, or northern, forests near the northern tree limit. However, latitude isn't the only thing that can limit trees. Even south of the Arctic Circle, drying winds, permafrost, and poor soils inhibit tree growth, leading some people to give the taiga label to any stunted forest. Denali National Park and Preserve has identified areas of the park as taiga. Squirrels, foxes, bears, weasels, wolves, martens, voles, ptarmigan, and moose are all taiga inhabitants.

Taiga

See also FOREST; PERMAFROST; TUNDRA

TEMPERATURE

TEMPERATURE To get a sense of how big Alaska is, consider the temperature variation around the state: in February, the average temperature in Barrow, in the Arctic, is −17.8°F, while Ketchikan in Southeast averages 33.9°F.

Alaska has at least three distinct climate zones. The arctic zone, which includes Barrow, is very dry with cool summers and cold winters. Ketchikan, and all of Southeast Alaska, lie in the maritime zone, where weather is relatively mild, very wet, and often stormy. Fairbanks lies in the relatively dry continental zone, where temperatures fluctuate widely between cold winters and warm to hot summers. Anchorage is in a transition zone, with a blend of maritime and continental weather.

Differences between the zones are due mostly to latitude and the effect of mountain ranges and oceans on climate. Northern latitudes are colder because the sun strikes the earth there at a low angle, so much of its heat energy is lost to the atmosphere. Even in summer, the sun skims around the arctic sky instead of crossing over it.

The coldest temperature ever recorded in Alaska was –80°F, measured January 23, 1971, at Prospect Creek, about two hundred miles north of Fairbanks. On June 27, 1915, Fort Yukon enjoyed Alaska's record high of 100°F.

When the wind is blowing, windchill temperatures are often reported. At 0°F, a ten-mile-per-hour wind can cause the temperature to feel like it's –21°F. Windchill temperatures are given to help people know when they could be at risk of frostbite. Even on still days, people create their own wind when snow machining, dogsledding, or simply walking.

Windchill doesn't affect whether or not the tires on your car will have a flat spot on the bottom after sitting out all night, causing you to drive to work on "square" tires, nor does windchill affect whether a vinyl car seat will shatter when you sit on it. But windchill does affect how quickly the car cools off after you park it, and how cold you feel bustling from the car to the nearest building.

TIDE   Pacific Northwest Coast Native peoples say that a very long time ago, the Old Woman Who Lived by the Cliff controlled the tides. She often left them high, covering up all the good food along the shoreline. Raven, who was always hungry, became angry with the woman. When she taunted him, he began poking her in the behind with sea urchin spines. Raven wouldn't quit until the old woman promised to let the Northland tide fall twice a day.

You might see ravens today picking up a meal at low tide—small crabs if the tide isn't very low, or maybe a fat sea cucumber when the tide is all the way out. Counting all of the state's islands and all of the bays, inlets, and straits, 47,000 miles of Alaska shoreline are washed by tides. An important and plentiful community of marine invertebrates lives along the tidal hem.

Rocky shorelines can have four distinct levels, or tide zones, each inhabited by specially adapted creatures. The uppermost level, called the splash zone, is constantly moistened by ocean spray but is underwater only at extreme high tides. In the splash zone, lichen, moss, and algae spread a welcome mat at the door of the next zone down, the high-tide zone.

Uncovered during most of a twenty-four-hour day, the high-tide zone is home to mostly hard-shelled creatures such as barnacles, limpets, and shore crabs. At the mid-tide zone, there is increased submersion time, so animals may forgo the hard shell needed in the more active and exposed wave zones; anemones and sea stars appear here. In the fourth zone, the low-tide zone, bottom dwellers are exposed to ravens and air only about twice a month. Nudibranchs live in the low-tide zone, as do sponges, sea cucumbers, and more anemones and sea stars.

Disregarding Raven and the Old Woman Who Lived by the Cliff, scientists determined that tides are controlled by the moon, 238,900 miles away, and to a lesser extent by the sun—an explanation nearly as fantastic as the Raven theory. Gravity causes the water in the ocean to rise (flood) and fall (ebb). As the moon orbits around the rotating earth, changing gravitational force causes intermittent bulges and troughs in the seas, which create the tides. Although the moon is the primary force causing the tides to ebb and flow, the secondary force of the sun's gravity causes tides to change in height every day.

Cook Inlet in Southcentral Alaska has the second-biggest tidal range in North America—an almost forty-foot difference between the highest high and lowest low. Nova Scotia's Bay of Fundy beats Cook Inlet by only about four feet.

> **Cook Inlet has the second-biggest tidal range in North America.**

Cook Inlet is a long, narrow body, so the water entering the inlet from the Pacific Ocean on a rising tide essentially has to squeeze in. Filling and draining a large volume of water into and out of a relatively small space keeps the waters of Cook Inlet in almost constant motion. Influenced by the earth's rotation, the inlet's tides flow counterclockwise: flooding in along the east side and ebbing out along the west.

Not surprisingly, Cook Inlet has a tidal bore—a foaming wall of water formed by a flood tide surging into a constricted inlet. Bores are most dramatic at Knik and Turnagain Arms (two smaller inlets branching off from the head of Cook Inlet), where water is compressed even further. Tides in Turnagain

Arm can produce bore tides up to six feet high, moving at speeds of up to ten knots. Even higher bore tides are whipped up when an unusually high tide comes in against a strong wind from the southeast. Turnagain Arm bore tides can sometimes be viewed along the Seward Highway, between twenty-six and thirty-seven miles south of Anchorage, about two hours and fifteen minutes later than the tide-book prediction for low tide at Anchorage.

TOR The craggy, isolated spires of granitic rock scattered around the high ground of Interior Alaska are called tors. More-famous tors loom over the moors of Devon and Cornwall in England, but Interior Alaska's tors, such as the hundred-foot-tall forms northeast of Fairbanks, are important in their own right as clues to the region's geologic history. The fact that these tors haven't been ground down by glaciers are a good indication that central Alaska escaped severe glaciation during the last ice age, and was therefore a refuge and migratory path for animals and plants.

A tor forms from an underground granite mass. Over time, temperature changes and other forces cause fractures in the granite to widen, breaking and cracking the granite into blocks, still buried in the earth. Eventually, weathering and erosion wear away the overlying earth layer, exposing the tor as a monument to the processes of time.

Once exposed, the tor continues to cleave. In Alaska, the most significant fracturing force comes from the repeated freezing and thawing of water that has seeped into cracks in the rock.

See also BERINGIA

TUNDRA Tundra is often described as barren and featureless. Tell that to the billions of insects, millions of flowers, hordes of rodents, interminable tussocks, and sporadic shrubs that are all tundra inhabitants.

Technically, "tundra" is a vegetation or habitat type. But the word is commonly used to refer to any northern, treeless moor with moisture-retaining soils and permanently frozen subsoil. Most of Alaska above the Arctic Circle and much of Alaska's

Interior region are covered by one of three distinct types of tundra: wet, moist, and alpine.

Large animals such as brown bears, caribou, and musk oxen roam tundra habitats, feeding on tundra grasses, sedges, and flowers. Despite its "empty" appearance, tundra habitat supports a diverse array of plants. They just aren't that noticeable because they are very small, having adapted to the harsh environment by keeping a low profile in the drying winds and freezing temperatures. Many flower and tree species grow in specialized dwarf tundra varieties—a whole bouquet of which might fit in a matchbox. Hundred-year-old tundra willows may be little taller than a ptarmigan.

> Most of Alaska above the Arctic Circle and much of the Interior are covered by tundra.

Practically every kind of tundra plant has a population of small to tiny invertebrates living around it, including springtails, beetles, midges, butterflies, bees, flies, mosquitoes, spiders, wasps, and mites. Insects may overwinter as eggs, larvae, or adults. Some Northland insect species, including some butterflies, produce their own forms of internal antifreeze to see them through the winter; others, such as snow fleas and the larvae of midges, have developed a metabolism that allows them to freeze and thaw several times with no ill effects.

From the vantage point of a small plane, some areas of tundra appear cracked and scoured like alligator skin, where expansion and contraction from constant freezing and thawing of the tundra's moisture-retaining soil have created giant polygonal patterns in the ground.

The flat or rolling tundra appears easy to traverse, but that's not necessarily true. Knobby, vegetated mounds called tussocks, found crowded together in moist (but not wet) tundra, make foot travel difficult. Walking on top of tussocks is like trying to walk across narrow, tipsy footstools; if you try to step across the grassy tops, you run the risk of falling off and breaking an ankle or twisting a knee. But weaving around them through the boggy ground is just as arduous.

See also BUTTERFLY; PERMAFROST; SNOW FLEA; TAIGA

VOLCANO One of the most impressive volcanic eruptions of recorded history turned a lush, forested valley of Southwest Alaska into the "moonscape" now known as Valley of Ten Thousand Smokes. The 1912 eruption of a then-unnamed volcano took sixty hours to spew an amount of ash and rock that could fill enough boxcars to circle the earth several times. Novarupta's explosion—fifty times greater than the 1980 eruption of Mount St. Helens—could be heard 750 miles away. Airborne debris darkened skies over much of the Northern Hemisphere for several days, and even when the skies cleared, debris clouds remained aloft, diminish-ing the warmth of the sun for months. In Kodiak, 100 miles from the volcano, houses collapsed under the weight of a foot or more of ash.

Novarupta and its close neighbor, Mount Katmai, are part of a chain of volcanoes strung from Southcentral Alaska to the Alaska Peninsula and Aleutian Islands. This chain is part of the Ring of Fire, a ring around the Pacific Ocean that marks where the earth's crustal plates push and grind against one another. From Southcentral Alaska through the Aleutians, the Pacific plate is actually sliding under the North American plate. Along

Mount Martin

with creating volcanoes, this plate activity also makes the area highly seismic, or prone to earthquakes.

Fifty miles deep in the earth under volcanoes, a combination of physical and chemical processes causes rock to melt. This molten rock, or magma, collects in an underground magma chamber. As pressure builds, magma swells out, looking for an escape. Gases begin to bubble out of the molten rock until their collective pressure blasts open an escape vent through which the gases, ash, and lava are ejected. In addition to the main center vent, vents may also open up on the volcano's flanks. Magma from the main chamber can also find its way up to "subsidiary cones" some distance from the main volcano.

Volcanic action in the Great Land isn't limited to the Valley of Ten Thousand Smokes. If you look across Cook Inlet from the Kenai Peninsula on a clear day, four active volcanoes are visible: Spurr, Redoubt, Iliamna, and Augustine. Augustine last erupted in 1986, disrupting air travel in the vicinity for several days. Activity on Mount Redoubt in 1989 and 1990 marked that volcano's eighth eruptive phase since 1700; ash from that eruption reached Fairbanks. Mount Spurr erupted in 1992; Anchorage received the brunt of the ash fallout from the August eruption, which halted air traffic out of the city for several days. A secondary eruption in September also briefly disrupted air traffic.

Alaska's largest active volcano, 14,163-foot Mount Wrangell, is visible from the Alaska Highway near Glennallen.

About eighty of Alaska's volcanoes are considered potentially active, 10 percent of the world's total. Volcanoes with the classic cone shape are most likely to be active because erosion alters the shape of extinct volcanoes in a relatively short time—geologically speaking, anyway.

See also EARTHQUAKE

WATERMELON SNOW It's as if Mother Nature uses Alaska's snow to blot her lipstick. Small, scattered patches of reddish pink "watermelon snow" are caused by algal growth. More than one hundred species of snow algae have been identified; most are red, but algae might also color the snow green, yellow, or even purple.

Neither plants nor animals, algae (placed in the kingdom Protoctista) can support themselves wherever there is light, carbon dioxide, oxygen, water, and a few minerals. The most common snow alga, *Chlamydomonas nivalis,* is a red-pigmented, single-celled organism with an eyespot, that propels itself with tail-like flagella. *C. nivalis* also contains chlorophyll and is capable of photosynthesis.

During the winter this alga may lie buried under the snow, but with the increasing light and wetness of spring, it migrates to the surface, collecting in tinted patches on melting snowbanks. As the only plant-like thing growing on the surface of an ice field, watermelon snow is a picnic ground for ice worms, spiders, and insects—who in turn become picnic fare for birds.

WAVE

Two kinds of waves make a big splash in Alaska: tsunami, or tidal wave, and seiche, or splash wave.

Although sometimes called tidal waves, tsunamis actually have nothing to do with tides; they are usually generated by undersea earthquakes or by volcanic eruptions that cause mass water movement. While still in the open ocean, tsunamis may travel at speeds of up to six hundred miles per hour. Even so, they are hardly noticeable, as the wave may stretch one hundred miles from crest to crest and only be a few feet high. Ships can sometimes feel tsunamis pass but are rarely damaged. The danger comes when this huge, fast wave approaches the shore and all the wave's force is packed into less water. The forward motion becomes restricted and the tsunami sort of falls forward on itself, transforming a two-foot-tall wave traveling at five hundred miles per hour in the open ocean to a hundred-foot-tall wall of water meeting the shore at thirty miles per hour.

> Tsunamis are usually generated by undersea earthquakes or volcanic eruptions.

Alaskans have experienced seven fatal tsunamis between 1788 and 1964. Tsunamis generated by the 1964 Good Friday earthquake destroyed three Alaska villages and also caused damage in Washington, Oregon, California, Chile, Hawaii, and Japan. Waves from a 1946 earthquake on Alaska's Unimak Island reached Hawaii within five hours, killing 159 people. Today, the Alaska Tsunami Warning Center in Palmer, Alaska, monitors undersea seismic activity, which has all but eliminated the danger of getting caught by surprise.

Where tsunamis originate underwater and are traveling waves, splash waves are typically generated by landslides and their movement consists of sloshing back and forth in a bay or lake. The biggest splash wave in recorded history occurred in 1958 near Yakutat when an earthquake caused forty million cubic yards of dirt and rocks to avalanche three thousand feet into Lituya Bay. The 100-foot-high splash wave caused by the landslide surged across the bay between 97 and 130 miles per hour and washed up the other side to a height of 1,740 feet—completely stripping the hillside of trees and soil. Four square miles of forest were destroyed.

See also EARTHQUAKE; TIDE

WETLAND Alaska has a big wet blanket; between 170 million and 233 million of the state's 365 million acres are wetlands: soggy meadows, wet tundra, marshes, river deltas, estuaries, mudflats, riparian areas (streamsides or lakesides), and potholes.

Wetlands occur throughout Alaska—from coastal river mouths in Southeast to Interior lowlands to potholes of the North Slope. A wetland can be anything from an area that is constantly flooded, such as a marsh, to a meadow with very wet soil that supports wetland plants like buckbean, marsh marigold, valerian, and wild iris.

Birds from nearly every continent travel here in the summer to feed and nest, drawn by the wetlands' abundant plant and insect food and hospitable ground-nesting sites. The 700,000-acre Copper River Delta—the largest uninterrupted wetland left on the Pacific Coast of North America—alone serves upwards of twenty million shorebirds and is considered the most important shorebird migratory rest stop in the Western Hemisphere. In addition, huge numbers of waterfowl use the extensive estuary,

Wetland with trumpeter swans

including nearly the entire world's population of dusky Canada geese and significant numbers of trumpeter swans.

In northeastern Alaska, the Yukon River Flats wetlands host one of the highest concentrations of nesting ducks in North America. At the other end of the Yukon, the Yukon–Kuskokwim Delta in Western Alaska attracts all of the world's cackling Canada geese, 90 percent of all emperor geese, and most of the Pacific population of tundra swans.

Birds aren't the only creatures who feed in Alaska's wetlands. Moose are often seen in wetlands grazing on aquatic plants; bears come for the berries, roots, grasses, and fish. Wolves and foxes enter wetlands to hunt the voles and other small rodents who live there.

Even though Alaska is rich in wetlands—harboring about 70 percent of our nation's remaining, rapidly dwindling wetland areas—habitat protection in the Lower 48 is still crucial to the millions of birds that use Alaska's wetlands. About two-thirds of the state's nesting birds migrate from somewhere else. Without safe and plentiful places to winter and to rest and feed during long migrations north, some avian populations could dwindle out—leaving all those Alaska mudflats, tide flats, estuaries, marshes, and wet tundra meadows feeling very empty.

See also MUSKEG

WHITEOUT AND ICE FOG No fancy names are

required for these climatological conditions: Alaskans just call them as they see them—or don't see, in these cases.

Whiteouts usually happen in blizzard situations, when strong surface winds blow snow around, although falling snow can also cause a whiteout. In a whiteout the horizon disappears, often accompanied by one's sense of equilibrium and depth—an especially unnerving feeling for skiers and drivers. Another form of whiteout familiar to Alaskans occurs when the ground is completely covered with snow (with no trees, houses, or other landmarks showing through) and the sky is overcast with featureless clouds. This type of whiteout is especially dangerous for pilots flying without the aid of instruments, as it becomes extremely difficult to perceive the distance to, or even direction of, the ground; many bush pilots have crashed under these circumstances.

Whereas whiteouts occur under nature's direction, ice fog is largely of our own making. The major source of ice fog is water vapor from automobile exhaust, the smokestacks of coal- and oil-fired power plants, woodstoves, furnace vents, and miscellaneous breathing. Ice fog is most common in towns located in valleys in colder parts of Alaska. Fairbanks is notorious for its ice fog, which settles over the town like a dim and eerie fog, so thick and close you can chuck a snowball farther than you can see. Visibility may be reduced to a few yards, making driving—and walking across the street—extremely dangerous. Strobe lights are mounted on the roofs of many Alaska school buses to make them more visible on ice fog days. Ice fog can occur naturally too, usually near a hot spring or other thermal feature that releases water vapor into cold air.

Ice fog forms because cold air cannot hold much water vapor. At room temperature, air can carry about twenty grams of water vapor per cubic meter, but at −40°F, the tolerance is two hundred times less. So, if air temperatures decrease while cars, homes, and power plants are pumping out extraneous moisture, the air just can't hold it all and water vapor materializes into ice crystals, which hang in the air as ice fog.

Temperature inversions can trap ice fog, sometimes for days on end. Inversions occur when a cooler layer of air near the ground is held down by a warmer layer of air above. Because temperatures near the ground in Northern Alaska are cold, and winds in the Interior are usually too light to disturb the layered air, inversions are very common.

The major source of ice fog is water vapor from automobile exhaust, smoke-stacks, and furnace vents.

Sulfur dioxide air pollution can be exacerbated by ice fog, but, interestingly, carbon monoxide levels are lower during ice fog than they are on some clear winter days when warm, dry air is moving northward over the Alaska Range, but the winds aren't reaching the ground.

WILDFIRE Alaska needs wildfire to balance its ice. In the Northland, a heavy buildup of accumulated vegetation can insulate the ground so well that the soil stays frozen, even in summer. Wildfires remove insulating layers of organic debris, and the blackened soil of a new burn absorbs great amounts of heat, so after a fire, warmth from the sun can penetrate the ground, thus helping to keep this permanently frozen ground, called "permafrost," from becoming established.

Wildfires also help replenish the topsoil. In moderate climates, dead vegetation lying on the ground breaks down relatively quickly, and nutrients are released into the soil. But in the colder parts of Alaska, decomposition is slow—until fire sweeps through. Fire disintegrates surface debris and makes the nutrients available to plants, breaking down proteins and other large molecules into forms plants can assimilate. After a fire, the amount of nitrogen, potassium, calcium, and phosphorus available to plants can increase significantly. Healthily sprouting shrubs, shoots, and grasses provide high-quality food for such animals as moose and bears.

Fires are a natural, constructive feature of the Alaskan landscape. All land management agencies present in the state—including the Bureau of Land Management, National Park

Service, Alaska Division of Forestry, Native corporations, and others—place their lands in one of four protection categories: critical, full, modified, and limited. Critical zones include populated areas and receive full protection. Fires in areas of limited protection are watched and managed, but are often allowed to burn if no property is threatened.

Because most of Alaska is roadless, transportation for firefighters and supplies is usually by airplane. Since heavy equipment can't easily be brought to most fire sites, Alaska's rough-and-ready firefighters—many of whom live in Alaska's bush villages—battle the blazes with shovels, chain saws, and pulaskis.

Most of Alaska's wildfires are started by lightning; during June thunderstorms, lightning may strike the Interior region as many as three thousand times in one day. Special computers detect ionization from lightning strikes anywhere in the state and plot their exact location; if the strike occurred in an area of concern, fire specialists may then fly out to evaluate the situation. The computer also reports which agency manages the land, and under which category of protection it lies.

Alaska's largest single fire occurred in the northwest part of the state in 1957, when more than one million acres burned. That year, 391 fires scorched a record five million acres. In the smoky summer of 2004 that record went up in flames, when 701 wildland fires burned nearly 6.6 million acres. Sixty percent of the largest fire years have occurred since 1990, with 2004 and 2005 being two of the three worst in 50 years.

See also PERMAFROST

WIND According to Greek mythology, the goddess Eurynome stirred the north wind to life by dancing; then the goddess and the wind made love. Three of their children live in Alaska: Chinook, Taku, and Williwaw.

Chinook winds begin as air sliding down the lee side of a mountain, warming up as it goes. The air is dry because moisture that may have been present earlier was shed as snow or rain on the trip up the windward side of the mountain. Outside Alaska, on the east slope of the Rocky Mountains, these warm, dry winds are often turbulent enough to reach the ground, where they seemingly inhale snow, evaporating up to an inch of snow an hour. Some Indian peoples of the American West called the winds "snow eaters." In Interior Alaska, chinook winds are generally so warm and buoyant that they don't reach all the way to the ground, but they are still welcome for the sunny, calm, and not-too-cold days they bring.

Taku winds, local to the Juneau area, are strong, sudden bursts of cold that sweep down from the Taku Glacier and Juneau Icefield. These frigid winds have been clocked at bone-chilling speeds of up to one hundred miles per hour.

Williwaws are violent winds usually associated with coastal mountains, where they funnel down the valleys to spill furiously out on the sea. Common to the Aleutian Islands and Western Alaska, williwaws often carry rain or snow, and are a bane to Alaskan mariners for their suddenness and turbulent gusts to 113 miles per hour. Whereas chinook winds are driven by large-scale winds in the atmosphere, williwaws are "katabatic" in nature—that is, driven by their own density. Williwaws are created when a mass of air is dammed up on the windward side of a mountain, then spills over in a sudden surge.

FURTHER READING

The Alaska Almanac: Facts About Alaska. Alaska Northwest Books

Alaska Department of Fish & Game Wildlife Notebook Series. Cheryl Hall, ed. ADF&G Public Communications Section, Juneau, 1994.

Alaska Science Nuggets, by Neil Davis, et al. University of Alaska Press, Fairbanks, 1989.

Alaska's History: The People, Land, and Events of the North Country, by Harry Ritter. Alaska Northwest Books, 1993.

Alaska's Mammals: A Guide to Selected Species, by Dave Smith. Alaska Northwest Books, 1995.

Alaska's Saltwater Fishes and Other Sea Life, by Doyne W. Kessler. Alaska Northwest Books, 1985.

Alaska Trees and Shrubs, by Leslie A. Viereck and Elbert L. Little, Jr. University of Alaska Press, Fairbanks, 1988.

Animals of the Arctic: The Ecology of the Far North, by Bernard Stonehouse. Holt, Rinehart & Winston, New York, 1971.

Cascade-Olympic Natural History: A Trailside Reference, by Daniel Mathews. Raven Editions/Portland Audubon Society, Portland, Oregon, 1988.

Discovering Wild Plants: Alaska, Western Canada, The Northwest, by Janice Schofield. Eaton Publishing, 2011.

The Freshwater Fishes of Alaska, by J. E. Morrow. Alaska Northwest Books, 1980.

Guide to the Birds of Alaska, 5th ed., by Robert H. Armstrong. Alaska Northwest Books, 2010.

It's Raining Frogs and Fishes: Four Seasons of Natural Phenomena and Oddities of the Sky, by Jerry Dennis. Harper/Collins, New York, 1992.

The Nature of Southeast Alaska: A Guide to Plants, Animals, and Habitats, by Rita M. O'Clair, Robert H. Armstrong, and Richard Carstensen. Alaska Northwest Books, 1992.

Roadside Geology of Alaska, by Cathy Connor and Daniel O'Haire. Mountain Press, Missoula, Montana, 1988.

Understanding the Aurora. Geophysical Institute, University of Alaska Fairbanks, 1991.

Wild, Edible, and Poisonous Plants of Alaska, by Christine Heller. Cooperative Extension Service, University of Alaska Fairbanks and the U.S.D.A., 1989.

INDEX

Illustrations are indicated by **bold** page numbers.

About the Author

Susan Ewing migrated to Alaska in 1974, and over a period of twelve years engaged in a variety of pursuits—from surveying parts of the Brooks Range, to a stint in Prudhoe Bay, to commercial fishing in Southeast—that allowed her to explore every region of the state. Her activities brought her into the company of whales, bears, salmon, moose, eagles, and the other wild lives that spark the heart of the Great Land.

She is also the author of *Going Wild in Washington and Oregon, The Great Rocky Mountain Nature Factbook,* and two children's books, *Lucky Hares and Itchy Bears* and *Ten Rowdy Ravens.* Her articles, essays, and short fiction have appeared in *Gray's Sporting Journal, Sports Afield, Big Sky Journal, Cowboys & Indians, Bugle,* and other publications and anthologies.

After leaving Alaska she settled in Montana, which is also a very beautiful place.